Natural Temptations

A Collection of Recipes from
The Junior League of
North Little Rock, Arkansas

THE NATURAL STATE

Natural Temptations

Copyright © 2001
Junior League of North Little Rock
P.O. Box 9043
North Little Rock, Arkansas 72119
501-372-1436

Library of Congress Number: 2001 135016
ISBN: 0-9709680-0-0

Designed, Edited, and Manufactured by
Favorite Recipes® Press
An imprint of

FRP™

P.O. Box 305142, Nashville, Tennessee 37230
1-800-358-0560

Art Director: Steve Newman
Designer: David Malone
Project Manager: Susan Larson

Manufactured in the United States of America
First Printing: 2001   12,500 copies

ON THE COVER

Compton Falls is just one of many exciting points along the Buffalo River, a federally-protected stream meandering through the Ozarks for almost 150 miles before joining the White River. Fill your canoe with a cooler of sodas, lunch, and snacks; put on your swimsuit, your life jacket, and your sunscreen. Grab an oar, and start paddling past towering limestone bluffs and through white-water rapids. If you're lucky, you might see a few elk grazing along the edge of the river. Elk or no elk, it will be a day you won't soon forget.

ACKNOWLEDGMENTS

Arkansas Department of Parks and Tourism

Danny Youngblood—Food Photographer

Amber Garrett—The visual coordinator/photographer for

the Arkansas Department of Parks and Tourism

A. C. Haralson—Scenic Photographer

Lynn Salmon for her vision for this cookbook

Debbie Horton—North Little Rock Junior League President 2000-2001

Gaye Long—North Little Rock Junior League President 2001-2002

Jan Pharo—Sustainer Advisor

ASSOCIATION OF JUNIOR LEAGUES
INTERNATIONAL MISSION STATEMENT

The Association of Junior Leagues International Inc. is an organization of women committed to promoting voluntarism, developing the potential of women and improving communities through the effective action and leadership of trained volunteers. Its purpose is exclusively educational and charitable.

THE JUNIOR LEAGUE OF NORTH LITTLE ROCK COOKBOOK COMMITTEE

Jan Pharo,
Sustainer Advisor

Karen Hall,
Chairperson

Heather Kingston

Lydia Palasota

Christi Shepard

Melissa Myers

Lisa Phillips

Ellen Weiner

RECIPE TESTERS

Shelby Churchwell	Rita Hogan	Jan Pharo
Bliss Dean	Heather Kingston	Lisa Phillips
Marilyn Eagan	Melissa Myers	Christi Shepard
Karen Greenlee	LeAnn Nannen	Ellen Weiner
Karen Hall	Jill Ogles	Dee Whalen
Kristin Hodge	Lydia Palasota	Janis Williams

A MESSAGE FROM THE PRESIDENT

We hope that you enjoy all of our recipes and that they bring you joy and good eating whether you're entertaining friends or preparing family meals. No matter what your preference, we have the perfect recipe to fit your needs: from the quick and easy for a busy family to entertaining guests at casual get-togethers or festive celebrations. We are certain that the recipes in this book will delight your friends and family with good food and special times.

Bon Appétit!

Gaye Long
President
Junior League of North Little Rock

TABLE OF CONTENTS

FOREWORD

With its history of service in North Little Rock approaching fifty-five years,
the Junior League of North Little Rock is an organization of women committed to
promoting volunteerism, developing the potential of women, and improving the community
through the effective action and leadership of trained volunteers.

Currently, members of the Junior League of North Little Rock give their time,
efforts, and leadership toward five projects that benefit the community. The money raised
from the sale of "Natural Temptations" will be used to further these projects.

Heaven's Loft, a signature project that began in 1999 in partnership with Baptist
Health Memorial Medical Center, provides a source of encouragement for low-income
expectant mothers and parents of young children to receive prenatal care, well baby care,
immunizations, and education. Parents are awarded a voucher when they keep preventative
maternity care, child care, or educational appointments. The earned vouchers can be
spent like cash on baby supplies in the Heaven's Loft store.

The League continues to partner with the Salvation Army to bring Christmas
to more than 1,400 children through the Salvation Army Angel Tree. More angels are
adopted from the Angel Tree staffed by the Junior League of North Little Rock
than from any other tree in Central Arkansas.

Each year members from the Junior League of North Little Rock teach five-year-olds how to safely cross the street and other important safety lessons before they begin the big world of kindergarten. The Safety Town project is presented in conjunction with St. Vincent's Infirmary Auxiliary.

League members demonstrate their support of historic preservation by giving their talents and energy to the improvement of the E. O. Manees House, located in historic downtown North Little Rock. Continuous improvements keep the house safe and beautiful to maintain its National Historic presence in the community and open to the public.

Junior League members also impact the community by giving hundreds of volunteer hours annually to area nonprofit organizations through its Community Bank project. This project also provides basic school supplies for North Pulaski County Middle Schools.

In 1979, the Junior League's first cookbook, "Rave Reviews," originated in the hearts and minds of our members. Twenty years and 35,000 copies later, we are proud to present a second cookbook, "Natural Temptations: A Collection of Recipes from The Junior League of North Little Rock."

Appetizers

THE OLD MILL

Watch carefully in the opening credits of the southern epic "Gone with the Wind" and you'll view a sight native to North Little Rock. The Old Mill, a re-creation of a water-powered grist mill, is now a bustling location for weddings, family pictures, and picnics. Adopted by groups like the North Little Rock Junior League and the Master Gardeners, wildflowers and greenery spring into life around the mill every spring, bringing with them visitors by the hundreds.

STUFFED ARTICHOKES

4 artichokes
1 loaf French bread
6 ounces Parmesan cheese, grated
1 garlic clove, crushed
Salt and pepper to taste
Olive oil

Rinse the artichokes and cut off the tips. Loosen the leaves and rinse again. Tear the French bread into pieces. Process in a food processor until fine crumbs form. Add the cheese and garlic. Process until combined. Season with salt and pepper. Stuff the artichokes with the bread mixture until full. Drizzle with olive oil. Add enough water to cover the bottom of a Dutch oven. Place the artichokes in the Dutch oven. Steam for 1 to 1 1/2 hours or until stuffing is moist and artichokes are dark green, adding water as needed.

Yield: 4 servings

TORTILLA ROLL-UPS

12 ounces cream cheese, softened
1/4 cup chopped green onions
1/2 cup shredded Cheddar cheese (optional)
1/4 cup chopped black olives (optional)
2 tablespoons chopped green chiles (optional)
1 (10-count) package large flour tortillas
Salsa

Combine the cream cheese, green onions, cheese, olives and chiles in a bowl and mix well. Spread evenly over the tortillas. Roll each tortilla up. Cut into 1/4- to 1/2-inch-thick slices. Serve with salsa.

Yield: 25 servings

MUSHROOM ROUNDS

1/2 cup (1 stick) butter, softened
3 ounces cream cheese, softened
1 cup flour
16 ounces fresh mushrooms, chopped
1 onion, chopped
3 tablespoons butter
Salt and pepper to taste
5 ounces cream cheese, softened

Combine 1/2 cup butter, 3 ounces cream cheese and flour in a bowl and mix well.
Shape into 24 balls. Place each ball in a miniature muffin cup and press over the
bottom and up the side. Sauté the mushrooms and onion in 3 tablespoons butter in a
skillet until tender. Season with salt and pepper. Add 5 ounces cream cheese and mix
well. Spoon into the prepared pastry. Bake at 375 degrees for 15 to 20 minutes or
until set. Serve warm.

Yield: 24 appetizers

STUFFED MUSHROOMS

32 ounces whole mushrooms
8 ounces cream cheese, softened
1 cup grated Parmesan cheese
1/2 cup chopped green onions
1/2 cup (1 stick) butter

Remove the stems from the mushrooms. Chop the mushroom stems. Combine 1/2 cup
of the chopped mushroom stems, cream cheese, Parmesan cheese and green onions in a
bowl and mix well. Reserve the remaining mushroom stems for another use. Sauté the
mushroom caps in the butter in a skillet. Stuff each mushroom cap with the cream
cheese mixture and place on a broiler pan. Broil until golden brown.

Yield: 8 to 10 servings

SHRIMP IN A PICKLE

3 pounds fresh shrimp

7 1/2 cups water

2 small purple onions, sliced

1 cup olive oil

1 cup red wine vinegar

3 tablespoons sugar

1 tablespoon grated
lemon zest

3 tablespoons fresh lemon juice

2 garlic cloves, pressed

1 tablespoon Dijon mustard

1 tablespoon white wine

Worcestershire sauce to taste

1 tablespoon hot sauce

1/2 teaspoon salt

1/2 cup chopped fresh basil

Cook the shrimp in the water in a saucepan until shrimp turn pink; drain. Arrange the shrimp over the bottom of a shallow airtight container. Arrange the onion slices over the shrimp. Whisk the olive oil, vinegar, sugar, lemon zest, lemon juice, garlic, Dijon mustard, wine, Worcestershire sauce, hot sauce, salt and basil together in a bowl. Pour over the onions. Chill, covered for 24 hours or longer, stirring occasionally. You may substitute thawed frozen cooked shrimp for the fresh shrimp and omit the step for cooking the shrimp.

Yield: 12 to 15 servings

CHEESE LOG

1 1/2 cups (or more) chopped pecans

24 ounces cream cheese, softened

1/2 (2 1/2-ounce) bottle Heinz 57 Steak Sauce

1/4 teaspoon garlic powder

1/4 cup Louisiana pepper sauce

Set aside a small amount of the chopped pecans. Beat the cream cheese, steak sauce, garlic powder and pepper sauce in a mixing bowl until smooth. Stir in the remaining pecans. Shape into a log. Roll in the reserved pecans to coat. Chill, covered, until firm.

Yield: 12 to 14 servings

CHOCOLATE CREAM CHEESE BALL

8 ounces cream cheese, softened
1/4 cup chocolate syrup
1/2 cup miniature chocolate chips

Combine the cream cheese and chocolate syrup in a bowl and mix well. Shape into a ball. Roll in the chocolate chips to coat. Chill, covered, until firm. Serve with graham crackers.

Yield: 4 to 6 servings

SHRIMP LOG

2 (4-ounce) cans shrimp
2 tablespoons chopped onion
8 ounces cream cheese, softened
1 tablespoon lemon juice
1 teaspoon horseradish powder
1/2 teaspoon salt
1/2 cup finely chopped pecans
1/2 cup parsley flakes

Drain the shrimp. Rinse and drain the shrimp. Place the shrimp in a bowl and mash. Add the onion, cream cheese, lemon juice, horseradish powder and salt and mix well. Shape into a log. Combine the pecans and parsley flakes in a shallow dish and mix well. Roll the shrimp log in the mixture to coat.

Yield: 6 to 8 servings

ANTIPASTO DIP

2 (4-ounce) jars button mushrooms, drained
1 (14-ounce) can artichoke hearts, drained, chopped
1 (3-ounce) jar stuffed green olives, drained
1 (4-ounce) jar sliced pimentos, drained
1/2 cup chopped bell pepper
1/2 cup chopped celery
1 small onion, chopped
1 teaspoon seasoned salt
1 teaspoon sugar
1 teaspoon MSG
1/4 cup minced onion
1/2 teaspoon seasoned pepper
1 teaspoon salt
1/2 teaspoon garlic salt
11/2 teaspoons onion salt
21/2 teaspoons Italian seasoning
2/3 cup white vinegar
1/3 cup vegetable oil
1 teaspoon chili powder

Combine the mushrooms, artichoke hearts, green olives, pimentos, bell pepper, celery and 1 small onion in a bowl and mix well.

Combine the seasoned salt, sugar, MSG, 1/4 cup onion, seasoned pepper, salt, garlic salt, onion salt, Italian seasoning, vinegar, oil and chili powder in a saucepan and mix well. Bring to a boil. Pour over the mushroom mixture. Serve with chips.

Yield: 8 to 10 servings

BROCCOLI DIP

3/4 cup (1$1/2$ sticks) butter
1 large onion, grated
1 (10-ounce) package frozen chopped broccoli
2 (10-ounce) cans cream of mushroom soup
1$1/2$ tubes garlic cheese
2 (4-ounce) cans mushrooms, drained
1 (2-ounce) package slivered almonds

Heat the butter in a saucepan over low heat until melted. Add the onion, broccoli, soup, cheese, mushrooms and almonds and mix well. Cook until heated through. Serve hot with chips.

Yield: 20 to 24 servings

COTTAGE CHEESE DIP

1 cup small curd cottage cheese
1 cup mayonnaise
2 teaspoons dillseed or dillweed
2 teaspoons Beau Monde seasoning
2 tablespoons minced onion
2 tablespoons chopped fresh parsley

Combine the cottage cheese, mayonnaise, dillseed, Beau Monde seasoning, onion and parsley in a bowl and mix well. Serve with chips.

Yield: 6 to 8 servings

CAVIAR PIE

CAVIAR PIE

8 ounces cream cheese, softened
1/4 cup mayonnaise
2 teaspoons minced or chopped onion
2 teaspoons Worcestershire sauce
2 teaspoons lemon juice
1 (2-ounce) jar black caviar
2 hard-cooked eggs, chopped
Chopped onion
Sliced lemons
Snipped parsley

Combine the cream cheese, mayonnaise, 2 teaspoons onion, Worcestershire sauce and lemon juice in a bowl and mix well. Spread over the center of a serving plate, smoothing the top. Chill until firm. Spoon the caviar over the center of the cream cheese mixture. Arrange the eggs and chopped onion around the caviar. Arrange the lemon slices around the eggs and onion. Sprinkle the parsley over the lemon slices.

Yield: 8 servings

QUICK AND EASY GUACAMOLE

3 black avocados
2 tablespoons lemon juice
1/2 teaspoon salt
1 1/2 teaspoons cumin
2 teaspoons garlic powder
1 tomato, seeded, finely chopped
1/2 small onion, finely chopped

Mash the avocados in a bowl. Add the lemon juice, salt, cumin and garlic powder and mix well; mixture will be slightly lumpy. Stir in the tomato and onion. Chill, covered, until ready to use.

Yield: 8 to 10 servings

HOT AND SPICY CORN DIP

1 (16-ounce) can yellow corn
1 (11-ounce) can white Shoe Peg corn
8 ounces cream cheese
1 (10-ounce) can tomatoes with green chiles
1 (4-ounce) can chopped green chiles
Chopped jalapeño chiles to taste
Garlic salt to taste
Cumin to taste

Combine the corn, cream cheese, tomatoes, green chiles, jalapeño chiles, garlic salt and cumin in a microwave-safe bowl. Microwave for 5 minutes or until cream cheese is melted, stirring occasionally. Serve warm with corn chips.

Yield: 15 to 20 servings

SHREDDED CHEESE DIP

1 cup sour cream
2 cups mayonnaise
2 cups shredded Cheddar cheese
1/2 cup chopped onion
6 tablespoons grated Parmesan cheese
1 teaspoon garlic powder
1 teaspoon seasoned salt
1/2 teaspoon pepper

Combine the sour cream, mayonnaise, Cheddar cheese, onion, Parmesan cheese, garlic powder, seasoned salt and pepper in bowl and mix well. Chill, covered, for 8 to 12 hours for enhanced flavor. Serve with crackers.

Yield: 15 to 20 servings

SPINACH DIP WITH PITA TOASTS

1 (10-ounce) package frozen spinach, thawed
1 tablespoon chopped jalapeño chiles
3/4 cup chopped onion
2 tomatoes, chopped
8 ounces cream cheese, softened
2 cups shredded Monterey Jack cheese
1/3 cup half-and-half
Pita Toasts

Drain the spinach, pressing out the excess moisture. Combine the spinach, jalapeño chiles, onion, tomatoes, cream cheese, Monterey Jack cheese and half-and-half in a bowl and mix well. Spoon into a buttered baking dish. Bake at 400 degrees for 20 to 25 minutes. Serve warm with Pita Toasts.

Yield: 10 to 12 servings

PITA TOASTS

1/2 cup (1 stick) butter, melted
2 teaspoons lemon pepper
2 teaspoons ground cumin
6 pita bread rounds

Combine the butter, lemon pepper and cumin in a shallow dish and mix well. Cut each pita bread round in half. Cut each half open and cut the pieces into triangles. Dip each piece into the butter mixture and place on a broiler pan. Broil until crisp.

SPINACH ARTICHOKE DIP

2 (14-ounce) cans artichoke hearts, drained, chopped
1 cup grated Parmesan cheese
1 (10-ounce) package frozen chopped spinach, thawed
1 teaspoon minced garlic
1 cup mayonnaise
Salt and black pepper to taste
Cayenne pepper
Paprika

Combine the artichoke hearts, cheese, spinach, garlic, mayonnaise, salt and black pepper in a bowl and mix well. Spoon into a 9×9-inch baking dish. Sprinkle with the cayenne pepper and paprika. Bake at 350 degrees until bubbly and light brown. Serve with crackers.

Yield: 8 to 10 servings

TZATZIKI DIP

1 small cucumber, grated
1 garlic clove, minced
1 (8-ounce) container plain yogurt
2 teaspoons lemon juice
1/2 teaspoon dried mint

Wrap the cucumber in cheesecloth, pressing to remove excess moisture. Combine the cucumber, garlic, yogurt, lemon juice and mint in a bowl and mix well. Serve with pita wedges.

Yield: 6 servings

MEXICAN TACO DIP

1¹/₂ pounds ground beef
1 envelope mild taco seasoning mix
16 ounces cream cheese, softened
1 (8-ounce) carton French onion dip
1 (8-ounce) jar salsa
3 cups shredded Cheddar and Monterey Jack cheese mixture

Brown the ground beef in a skillet, stirring until crumbly; drain. Prepare the taco mix following the package directions and using the browned ground beef. Combine the cream cheese and French onion dip in a bowl and mix well. Layer the cream cheese mixture, ground beef mixture, salsa and cheeses over the bottom of a 9×13-inch baking dish. Bake, covered, at 350 degrees for 20 to 30 minutes or until heated through. Serve with taco chips or tortillas.

Yield: 25 to 30 servings

PEPPERONI DIP

1 cup sour cream
8 ounces cream cheese, softened
¹/₃ cup grated Parmesan cheese
1¹/₂ teaspoons garlic powder
1 (14-ounce) jar pizza sauce
2 cups shredded mozzarella cheese
3 ounces pepperoni, chopped

Combine the sour cream, cream cheese, Parmesan cheese and garlic powder in a bowl and mix well. Spread over the bottom of a pie plate. Pour the pizza sauce evenly over the cream cheese mixture. Sprinkle the mozzarella cheese over the sauce. Sprinkle the pepperoni over the top. Bake at 350 degrees until bubbly.

Yield: 16 to 20 servings

SHRIMP DIP

8 ounces cream cheese, softened
1 cup sour cream
2 tablespoons mayonnaise
2 or 3 (4-ounce) cans shrimp
2 teaspoons lemon juice
1/4 cup chopped green onions
Dash of garlic
Dash of salt
Dash of pepper

Combine the cream cheese, sour cream, mayonnaise, shrimp, lemon juice, green onions, garlic, salt and pepper in a bowl and mix well. Chill, covered, in the refrigerator. Serve with crackers.

Yield: 10 to 12 servings

BANANA SALSA

1/2 cup chopped green bell pepper
1/2 cup chopped yellow bell pepper
1/2 cup chopped red bell pepper
3 green onions, chopped
1 tablespoon chopped fresh cilantro
2 tablespoons light brown sugar
3 tablespoons fresh lime juice
1 tablespoon vegetable oil
1/4 teaspoon salt
1/4 teaspoon pepper
1 small jalapeño chile, seeded, chopped
2 bananas, chopped

Combine the bell peppers, green onions, cilantro, brown sugar, lime juice, oil, salt and pepper in a bowl and mix well. Stir in the jalapeño chile. Stir in the bananas. Chill, covered, for 3 hours.

Yield: 8 servings

BLACK BEAN SALSA

2 tomatoes, seeded, chopped
1/2 cup chopped green onions
2 tablespoons snipped fresh cilantro
3 garlic cloves, minced
2 tablespoons lime juice
1 (15-ounce) can black beans, rinsed, drained
1/4 teaspoon salt
1/8 teaspoon pepper

Combine the tomatoes, green onions, cilantro and garlic in a bowl and mix well. Add the lime juice, black beans, salt and pepper and mix gently. Chill, covered, for 1 to 2 hours.

Yield: 12 to 15 servings

FRESH TOMATO SALSA

5 tomatoes, finely chopped
1 purple onion, finely chopped
4 green onions, chopped
1 (4-ounce) can chopped green chiles
1/2 cup vinegar
1/2 cup dried parsley
2 garlic cloves, minced
1/2 teaspoon oregano
1 teaspoon cumin
2 tablespoons olive oil
Salt and pepper to taste
Tabasco sauce to taste

Combine the tomatoes, purple onion, green onions, green chiles, vinegar, parsley, garlic, oregano, cumin, olive oil, salt, pepper and Tabasco sauce in a bowl and mix well. Chill, covered, for 8 hours or longer.

Yield: 15 to 20 servings

Beverages

BUFFALO RIVER

The Buffalo River, the first in the country to be protected by Congress as a free-flowing stream, provides a variety of recreational opportunities. Camp outside or rest in style in a nearby cabin, greet the morning sunrise and head out to the river to float all day, warmed by the Arkansas summer sun. There's no better way to spend a Saturday. Flowing through 132 miles of the most spectacular section of the Arkansas Ozarks highlands, the Buffalo displays multi-colored bluffs towering 500 feet or more above the water, lofty waterfalls, massive boulders, hairpin turns, and unforgettable beauty and charm. Try it once and you'll make it a regular part of your summer routine.

CHRISTMAS RUM PUNCH

1 (64-ounce) can cranberry juice cocktail
4 cups light rum
4 cups ginger ale

Combine the cranberry juice cocktail, rum and ginger ale in a large container and mix well. Chill until ready to serve. Pour into a punch bowl.

Yield: 32 (1/2-cup) servings

EASY PARTY PUNCH

1 (46-ounce) can pineapple juice
1 (2-liter) bottle lemon-lime soda
1 (5-ounce) package sugar-sweetened cherry
or raspberry drink mix

Combine the pineapple juice, soda and drink mix in a large container and mix well. Serve chilled or over ice. You may serve this with sherbet.

Yield: 28 (1/2-cup) servings

GOLDEN PUNCH

2 (6-ounce) cans frozen orange juice concentrate
2 (6-ounce) cans frozen lemonade concentrate
2 (46-ounce) cans pineapple juice
1/3 cup sugar, or to taste
4 cups ginger ale

Prepare the orange juice concentrate using the package directions. Prepare the lemonade concentrate using the package directions. Combine the prepared orange juice, prepared lemonade, pineapple juice and sugar in a large container and mix well. Chill for 8 to 12 hours. Pour into a punch bowl just before serving. Stir in the ginger ale.

Yield: 44 (1/2-cup) servings

HOLIDAY CITRUS PUNCH

4 cups cranberry juice cocktail
1 (6-ounce) can frozen orange juice concentrate, thawed
1 (6-ounce) can frozen lemonade concentrate, thawed
2 cups water
1 3/4 cups ginger ale
Orange slices for garnish

Combine the cranberry juice cocktail, orange juice concentrate, lemonade concentrate and water in a container and mix well. Chill until ready to serve. Pour into a punch bowl. Stir in the ginger ale. Garnish with orange slices.

Yield: 18 (1/2-cup) servings

SLUSHY PUNCH

1 (6-ounce) package gelatin, flavor of choice
1/2 cup sugar
2 cups boiling water
1 (46-ounce) can pineapple juice
1 (12-ounce) can frozen orange juice concentrate
1 (12-ounce) can frozen lemonade concentrate
6 cups cold water
4 cups ginger ale

Dissolve the gelatin and sugar in the boiling water in a large container. Add the pineapple juice, orange juice concentrate, lemonade concentrate and cold water and mix well. Pour into a freezer container. Freeze until slushy. Spoon into a punch bowl. Stir in the ginger ale.

Note: Use a gelatin flavor that is the color you want your punch to be. For peach-colored punch use apricot gelatin, for red-colored punch use grape gelatin or for a pink-colored punch use mixed fruit gelatin.

Yield: 40 (1/2-cup) servings

STRAWBERRY PUNCH

2 (5-ounces) packages unsweetened strawberry drink mix
$1^1/2$ cups sugar
1 (46-ounce) can pineapple juice
1 (2-liter) bottle lemon-lime soda or ginger ale

Dissolve the drink mixes and the sugar in the pineapple juice in a freezer container. Freeze until frozen through. Let stand at room temperature for 2 hours. Stir in the soda; punch will be slushy.

Yield: 32 (1/2-cup) servings

RASPBERRY CHAMPAGNE PUNCH

1 (6-ounce) can frozen lemonade concentrate
1 cup water
1 (10-ounce) package frozen raspberries
1 (1-liter) bottle lemon-lime soda, chilled
1 large bottle champagne, chilled

Dissolve the lemonade concentrate in the water in a large container. Stir in the raspberries, soda and champagne gently. Pour into a punch bowl.

Yield: 18 to 20 servings

STRAWBERRY SENSATION

3 (6-ounce) packages strawberry gelatin
4 cups sugar
9 cups boiling water
2 (64-ounce) cans pineapple juice
1 (16-ounce) bottle lemon juice
5 (10-ounce) cartons sliced sweetened frozen strawberries
5 (2-liter) bottles lemon-lime soda

Dissolve the gelatin and sugar in the boiling water in a large container. Let cool. Add the pineapple juice and lemon juice. Place the strawberries from each carton into a sealable plastic freezer bag. Divide the punch equally among the bags; each bag should be 1/2 to 3/4 full. Seal the bags and freeze. Remove the bags from the freezer. Let stand at room temperature until partially thawed. Combine with the soda in a punch bowl; punch will be slushy. You may thaw the bags one at a time and combine with 2 liters of lemon-lime soda.

Yield: 150 (1/2-cup) servings

PARTY PUNCH

PARTY PUNCH

1 (6-ounce) can frozen
lemonade concentrate, thawed
1 (5-ounce) package sweetened
drink mix, flavor of choice
1 (64-ounce) can
pineapple juice

1 (64-ounce) can orange juice
1 (2-liter) bottle
lemon-lime soda
2 cups water (optional)
1 fifth rum (optional)
Ice Ring (optional)

Combine the lemonade concentrate and drink mix in a large container and mix well. Stir in the pineapple juice, orange juice, lemon-lime soda, water and rum. Pour over Ice Ring in a punch bowl.

Yield: 50 (1/2-cup) servings

ICE RING

Fruit pieces or edible flowers of choice

Pour enough water into a ring mold to fill halfway. Freeze until solid. Arrange pieces of fruit or edible fresh flowers or greenery on the ice. Freeze until solid. Add enough cold water to the mold to fill. Freeze for 8 to 12 hours. Unmold into a punch bowl.

BOURBON SLUSH

2 cups water
1 large tea bag
1 cup sugar
2 cups bourbon
1 (12-ounce) can frozen
lemonade concentrate

1 (6-ounce) can frozen orange
juice concentrate
6 cups cold water
1 (3-liter) bottle
lemon-lime soda

Bring 2 cups water to a boil in a small saucepan. Steep the tea bag in the water. Combine tea, sugar, bourbon, lemonade concentrate, orange juice concentrate and cold water in a freezer container and mix well. Freeze for 24 hours. Add the soda to the bourbon mixture and mix well. Spoon into a punch bowl.

Yield: 50 (1/2-cup) servings

NONALCOHOLIC PINA COLADAS

1 (12-ounce) can evaporated skim milk
1 (8-ounce) can pineapple chunks
1/2 cup frozen pineapple-orange juice concentrate
1 large banana, sliced
1/2 teaspoon rum extract
1/2 teaspoon coconut extract

Process the milk, pineapple, orange juice concentrate, banana, rum extract and coconut extract in a blender until smooth. Add enough ice to measure 5 cups. Process until smooth.

Yield: 5 (1-cup) servings

ROYAL EGGNOG

2 quarts vanilla ice cream
4 cups hot strong coffee
4 cups blended whiskey
1 cup light rum
Grated nutmeg

Combine the ice cream and coffee in a punch bowl and stir until ice cream melts. Stir in the whiskey and rum. Sprinkle the nutmeg over the top.

Yield: 32 (1/2-cup) servings

VODKA SLUSH

1 (4-ounce) jar maraschino cherries
1 (6-ounce) can frozen orange juice concentrate
3/4 cup water
1 (46-ounce) can pineapple juice
2 cups vodka
1 cup sugar
1 (2-liter) bottle lemon-lime soda

Drain the cherries, reserving the juice. Combine the reserved juice, orange juice concentrate, water, pineapple juice, vodka, sugar and soda in a large freezer container and mix well. Freeze for 3 to 4 hours or until slushy. Stir in the cherries. Freeze for 8 to 12 hours. Serve frozen.

Yield: 35 (1/2-cup) servings

WHISKEY SOURS

1 (6-ounce) can frozen lemonade concentrate, thawed
1/2 (6-ounce) can frozen orange juice concentrate, thawed
1 1/2 cups bourbon
1 cup water
1 1/2 cups carbonated beverage

Combine the lemonade concentrate, orange juice concentrate, bourbon, water and carbonated beverage in a container and mix well. Serve over ice.

Yield: 4 (1-cup) servings

CINNAMON MINT TEA

6 cups water
1 family-size tea bag
2 cinnamon sticks
Mint leaves for garnish

Bring the water to a boil in a saucepan. Remove from the heat. Place the tea bag in the water and cover the saucepan. Steep the tea bag for 5 to 10 minutes. Remove the tea bag. Stir the tea with the cinnamon sticks. Set the cinnamon sticks in the tea. Pour the tea over ice in tea glasses. Garnish with a mint leaf.

Yield: 12 (1/2-cup) servings

SPICED TEA MIX

1 (18-ounce) jar orange drink mix
$1^1/4$ cups sugar
$3/4$ cup instant tea
1 teaspoon cinnamon
1/2 teaspoon ground cloves
Dash of salt

Combine the drink mix, sugar, tea, cinnamon, cloves and salt in an airtight container and mix well. Combine 3 to 4 teaspoons with 1 cup hot water in a mug and mix well.

Yield: Variable

CAFE MOCHA MIX

1 cup instant coffee
1/2 cup baking cocoa
1/2 cup nondairy creamer
12 tablespoons confectioners' sugar

Combine the coffee, baking cocoa, creamer and confectioners' sugar in an airtight container and mix well. Combine 1 to 2 tablespoons with 1 cup of boiling water in a mug and mix well.

Yield: 30 servings

INSTANT HOT CHOCOLATE

32 ounces chocolate drink mix
11 ounces nondairy creamer
1 (16-ounce) package confectioners' sugar
1 (8-quart) box instant dry milk

Combine the drink mix, creamer, sugar and dry milk in an airtight container and mix well. Place enough of the hot chocolate mix in a mug to fill halfway. Add enough hot water to fill and mix well.

Yield: Variable

Breads and Brunch

LAKE CATHERINE

Lake Catherine is one of five diamond lakes serving up thousands of acres of sparkling recreational waters and countless miles of shoreline fun. Lake Catherine is beautiful, secluded, and a popular setting for bass fishing and water sports. Campsites, cabins, a restaurant, a marina, and hiking trails are located at nearby Lake Catherine State Park. The 2,000-acre lake, formed by the 1924 creation of Remmel Dam, was named after the only daughter of Harvey Couch of Magnolia, the man who brought electricity to Arkansas.

CRANBERRY BANANA BREAD

1 cup sugar	2 eggs
1/2 cup (1 stick) butter, softened	2 cups flour
	2 teaspoons baking powder
1 cup mashed banana	1/2 cup chopped walnuts
1/4 cup milk	1 1/4 cups craisins

Cream the sugar and butter in a mixing bowl until light and fluffy. Add the banana, milk and eggs and mix well. Add the flour and baking powder and mix just until moistened. Stir in the walnuts and craisins. Spoon the batter evenly into a greased 5×9-inch loaf pan. Bake at 350 degrees for 1 hour or until a wooden pick inserted in the center comes out clean. Cool in the pan for 10 minutes. Remove to a wire rack to cool completely.

Yield: 1 loaf

PUMPKIN BREAD

3 1/2 cups flour	3 cups sugar
2 teaspoons baking soda	1 cup shortening or vegetable oil
1 teaspoon (heaping) nutmeg	
1 1/2 teaspoons salt	4 eggs
1 (30-ounce) can pumpkin	2/3 cup water

Sift the flour, baking soda, nutmeg and salt together. Combine the pumpkin, sugar, shortening and eggs in a bowl and mix well. Add the sifted dry ingredients alternately with the water, mixing well after each addition. Pour into 2 large loaf pans. Bake at 350 degrees for 1 hour and 15 minutes. Cool in the pan for 10 minutes. Remove to a wire rack. Serve warm or cold.

Yield: 2 loaves

SAUSAGE BREAD

1 pound bulk pork sausage
1 (3-ounce) package sliced
    pepperoni
1 large white onion,
    finely chopped
1 large bell pepper,
    finely chopped

1/4 cup (1/2 stick) butter
2 tablespoons oregano
1 tablespoon garlic powder
8 ounces mozzarella cheese,
    shredded
2 (1-pound) loaves frozen
    bread dough, thawed

Brown the sausage in a skillet, stirring until crumbly; drain. Microwave the pepperoni for 45 seconds. Sauté the onion and bell pepper in the butter in a skillet until tender. Combine the cooked sausage, pepperoni, onion, bell pepper, oregano, garlic powder and cheese in a bowl and mix well.

Roll each loaf of bread dough into a thin rectangle. Spread the sausage mixture over the dough. Roll as for a jelly roll, sealing the edge and ends. Place the loaves on a baking sheet. Bake at 350 degrees for 20 minutes. Spread butter over the tops. Cut into 3/4-inch-thick slices.

Yield: 2 loaves

VEGETABLE BREAD

3 (10-count) cans biscuits
3/4 cup chopped onion
3/4 cup chopped green or red
    bell pepper
3/4 cup chopped celery

1 cup (2 sticks) butter
3/4 cup shredded Cheddar or
    grated Parmesan cheese
8 ounces bacon, crisp-cooked,
    crumbled

Cut the biscuits into quarters. Place in a large bowl. Sauté the onion, bell pepper and celery in the butter in a skillet for 5 to 10 minutes or until tender. Add the cooked vegetables, cheese and bacon to the biscuit dough and toss to combine. Spoon into a bundt pan. Bake at 350 degrees for 30 to 35 minutes or until biscuits are brown. Invert onto a serving plate.

Yield: 12 to 16 servings

MEXICAN CORN BREAD

MEXICAN CORN BREAD

1 onion, chopped
Butter
1 cup cornmeal
1/2 teaspoon baking soda
1 teaspoon salt
1 (17-ounce) can cream-style corn
3/4 cup milk
1/3 cup margarine, melted
3 eggs
1 cup shredded Cheddar cheese

Grease a 9X9-inch baking pan. Place in a 400-degree oven. Sauté the onion in a small amount of butter in a skillet until tender. Combine the cornmeal, baking soda and salt in a bowl and mix well. Combine the corn, milk, margarine and eggs in a separate bowl and mix well. Stir in the cornmeal mixture. Layer 1/2 of the batter, 1/2 of the cheese, the onion, the remaining batter and the remaining cheese in the hot baking pan. Bake at 400 degrees for 45 minutes.

Yield: 9 servings

BROCCOLI CORN BREAD

1 cup (2 sticks) butter
4 eggs
1 (10-ounce) package frozen chopped broccoli, thawed
1 onion, chopped
1 cup cottage cheese
2 (8-ounce) packages corn bread mix

Place the butter in a 9X13-inch baking dish. Heat in a 375-degree oven until melted. Remove from the oven. Combine the eggs, broccoli, onion, cottage cheese and corn bread mixes in a bowl and mix well. Pour in the melted butter and mix well; do not scrape the baking dish. Spoon the corn bread mixture into the baking dish. Bake at 375 degrees for 30 to 40 minutes or until light brown.

Yield: 15 servings

REFRIGERATOR ROLLS

2 envelopes dry yeast
1 cup warm water
3/4 cup sugar
1/2 cup (1 stick) butter, softened

1 cup boiling water
2 egg whites
2 egg yolks
6 cups flour
1 teaspoon salt

Dissolve the yeast in the warm water. Cream the sugar and butter in a mixing bowl until light and fluffy. Add the boiling water and mix well. Cool to lukewarm. Beat the egg whites in a mixing bowl until stiff peaks form.

Stir the yeast and egg yolks into the sugar mixture. Add the flour and salt and mix well. Fold in the egg whites. Chill, covered, for 2 hours or longer.

Roll the dough 1/2 inch thick on a lightly floured surface. Cut with a round cutter. Place rolls on a greased baking sheet. Let rise until doubled in bulk. Bake at 350 degrees for 15 to 20 minutes or until light brown.

Yield: 3 dozen rolls

GREEK CRESCENTS

2 1/2 cups flour
1 cup (2 sticks) margarine, softened
1 egg yolk
1/2 teaspoon baking powder

1/4 cup sugar
2 tablespoons brandy
1/2 cup chopped pecans
Confectioners' sugar

Combine the flour, margarine, egg yolk, baking powder, sugar and brandy in a bowl and mix well. Stir in the pecans. Drop by tablespoonfuls onto a baking sheet. Shape into crescents. Bake at 375 degrees for 25 minutes. Cool slightly on a wire rack. Roll the warm crescents in the confectioners' sugar to coat.

Yield: 12 to 15 crescents

CHEESE GARLIC DROP BISCUITS

2 cups baking mix
1/4 teaspoon garlic powder
1/4 cup (1/2 stick) cold margarine
2 cups shredded Cheddar cheese
1/2 cup milk
1 tablespoon margarine
1 tablespoon grated Parmesan cheese
1/4 teaspoon parsley

Combine the baking mix and garlic powder in a bowl and mix well. Cut in 1/4 cup margarine until crumbly. Add the Cheddar cheese and milk, mixing just until combined. Drop by tablespoonfuls onto a greased baking sheet. Bake at 425 degrees until golden brown.

Heat 1 tablespoon margarine in a skillet until melted. Stir in the Parmesan cheese and parsley. Dip the top of each biscuit in the butter mixture.

Yield: 12 biscuits

RED HOT BISCUITS

2 3/4 cups baking mix
1/2 teaspoon crushed red pepper
1/2 teaspoon garlic powder
1 cup milk
1 cup shredded Cheddar cheese
2 tablespoons butter, melted
1/4 teaspoon garlic powder

Combine the baking mix, red pepper and 1/2 teaspoon garlic powder in a bowl and mix well. Add the milk and cheese, stirring with a fork until mixture forms a soft dough. Drop by 1/4 cupfuls onto a greased baking sheet. Combine the butter and 1/4 teaspoon garlic powder in a bowl and mix well. Brush over the tops of the biscuits. Bake at 425 degrees for 10 to 12 minutes or until golden brown.

Yield: 12 biscuits

HUSH PUPPIES

2 eggs
1 (8-ounce) can cream-style corn
2 green onions, minced
1 (9-ounce) package cornmeal mix
Vegetable oil for frying

Combine the eggs, corn and green onions in a bowl and mix well. Stir in enough cornmeal mix to make a soft dough. Drop by spoonfuls into hot deep oil (375-degree oil). Deep-fry until golden brown on all sides.

Yield: 6 to 8 servings

RAISIN BRAN MUFFINS

1 (10-ounce) package Raisin Bran
5 cups flour
3 cups sugar
5 teaspoons baking soda
2 teaspoons salt
4 cups buttermilk
1 cup vegetable oil
4 eggs

Combine the Raisin Bran, flour, sugar, baking soda, salt, buttermilk, oil and eggs in a bowl and mix just until combined. Fill greased muffin cups 2/3 full. Bake at 400 degrees for 15 to 20 minutes or until golden brown. You may keep the muffin batter in the refrigerator for up to 6 weeks.

Yield: 5 dozen

CARAMEL NUT ROLLS

1/2 cup (1 stick) butter or
margarine
1 cup packed brown sugar
1/2 cup chopped nuts

2 (10-count) cans refrigerator
biscuits
Cinnamon

Heat the butter in a saucepan until melted. Combine the brown sugar and nuts in a bowl and mix well. Dip each biscuit in the butter to coat. Roll in the brown sugar mixture. Layer the biscuits in a 2-pound coffee can, sprinkling cinnamon between each layer. Place the can in a slow-cooker. Place 8 paper towels over the top of the can. Place the lid on the slow cooker. Cook on High for 2 1/2 to 3 1/2 hours; do not check for at least 2 hours.

Yield: 10 servings

FRENCH BREAKFAST PUFFS

1 1/2 cups flour
1 1/2 teaspoons baking powder
1/2 teaspoon salt
1/4 teaspoon nutmeg
1/3 cup shortening
1/2 cup sugar

1 egg
1/2 cup milk
1/2 cup sugar
1 teaspoon cinnamon
6 tablespoons butter, melted

Sift the flour, baking powder, salt and nutmeg together. Cream the shortening and 1/2 cup sugar in a mixing bowl until light and fluffy. Add the egg and mix well. Add the sifted dry ingredients alternately with the milk, mixing well after each addition. Fill greased muffin cups 2/3 full. Bake at 350 degrees for 20 to 25 minutes or until golden brown.

Combine 1/2 cup sugar and cinnamon in a bowl and mix well. Roll the hot muffins in the melted butter. Roll in the cinnamon-sugar to coat.

Yield: 8 to 12 puffs

BLUEBERRY COFFEE CAKE

3 cups flour
$1^1/2$ teaspoons baking soda
$1^1/2$ teaspoons baking powder
3/4 teaspoon salt
1 cup sugar
3/4 cup ($1^1/2$ sticks) margarine, softened
$1^1/2$ teaspoons vanilla extract
3 eggs
$1^1/2$ cups sour cream
2 (21-ounce) cans blueberry pie filling
Brown Sugar Topping

Sift the flour, baking soda, baking powder and salt in a bowl and mix well. Cream the sugar and margarine in a mixing bowl until light and fluffy. Beat in the vanilla and eggs. Add the sifted dry ingredients alternately with the sour cream, mixing well after each addition. Layer the batter and pie filling half at a time in a greased 9×13-inch baking pan. Sprinkle Brown Sugar Topping over the layers. Bake at 350 degrees for 1 hour.

Yield: 15 servings

BROWN SUGAR TOPPING

1/3 cup packed brown sugar
1/2 cup sugar
1 teaspoon cinnamon
$1^1/2$ cups pecans

Combine the brown sugar, sugar, cinnamon and pecans in a bowl and mix well.

BLUEBERRY POPPY SEED BRUNCH CAKE

1¹/₂ cups flour
2 tablespoons poppy seeds
¹/₂ teaspoon baking soda
¹/₄ teaspoon salt
²/₃ cup sugar
¹/₂ cup (1 stick) butter or margarine, softened
2 teaspoons grated lemon zest
1 egg
¹/₂ cup sour cream
2 cups blueberries, drained
¹/₃ cup sugar
2 teaspoons flour
¹/₄ teaspoon nutmeg
Glaze

Combine 1¹/₂ cups flour, poppy seeds, baking soda and salt in a bowl and mix well. Cream ²/₃ cup sugar and butter in a mixing bowl until light and fluffy. Add the lemon zest and egg and mix well. Beat 2 minutes at medium speed. Add the flour mixture alternately with the sour cream, mixing well after each addition. Spread the batter over the bottom and 1 inch up the sides of a greased and floured 9- or 10-inch springform pan; batter must be ¹/₄ inch thick on the side.

Combine the blueberries, ¹/₃ cup sugar, 2 teaspoons flour and nutmeg in a bowl and mix well. Spoon over the batter.

Bake at 350 degrees for 45 to 55 minutes or until crust is golden brown. Cool slightly on a wire rack. Remove the side of the pan. Drizzle Glaze over the warm cake.

Yield: 8 servings

GLAZE

¹/₃ cup confectioners' sugar
1 to 2 teaspoons milk

Combine the confectioners' sugar and enough milk to make of the desired consistency in a bowl and mix until smooth.

COFFEE CAKE

1 (2-layer) package yellow cake mix
1 (4-ounce) package vanilla instant pudding mix
1/4 cup sugar
3/4 cup water
3/4 cup vegetable oil
4 eggs
1 teaspoon imitation butter flavoring
1 teaspoon vanilla extract
1 cup chopped pecans
2 teaspoons cinnamon
Butter Icing

Combine the cake mix, pudding mix, sugar, water, oil, eggs, butter flavoring and vanilla in a bowl and mix until smooth and creamy. Pour 1/2 of the batter into a bundt pan. Sprinkle with 1/2 of the pecans and 1/2 of the cinnamon. Pour the remaining batter over the pecans. Sprinkle the remaining pecans and remaining cinnamon over the batter. Bake at 350 degrees for 50 minutes. Cool in the pan for 10 minutes. Invert onto a serving plate. Drizzle Butter Icing over the cake.

Yield: 16 servings

BUTTER ICING

1 cup confectioners' sugar
3 tablespoons milk
1/2 teaspoon imitation butter flavoring
1/2 teaspoon vanilla extract

Combine the confectioners' sugar, milk, butter flavoring and vanilla in a bowl and mix until smooth.

CORNMEAL PANCAKES

1¹/4 cups cornmeal
2 tablespoons vegetable oil
1 tablespoon sugar
1 egg
1 teaspoon baking powder
Milk

Combine the cornmeal, oil, sugar, egg and baking powder in a bowl and mix well. Add enough milk to make of the desired consistency. Pour ¹/4 cup at a time onto a 350-degree griddle. Cook until brown on both sides, turning once. Serve with butter.

Yield: 3 or 4 servings

BREAKFAST PIZZA

1 (8-count) package crescent rolls
1 pound bulk sausage
4 ounces Cheddar cheese, shredded
1 cup frozen hash brown potatoes, or shredded potatoes
5 eggs, beaten
1/2 cup milk
Salt and pepper to taste

Unroll the crescent roll dough. Press over the bottom of a greased pizza pan, pressing the perforations to seal. Brown the sausage in a skillet, stirring until crumbly; drain. Layer the cooked sausage, cheese and potatoes over the dough. Combine the eggs, milk, salt and pepper in a bowl and mix well. Pour over the layers. Bake at 375 degrees for 20 to 30 minutes or until set.

Yield: 6 servings

BRUNCH EGG CASSEROLE

1/4 cup (1/2 stick) butter
1/4 cup flour
1 cup milk
1 cup light cream
12 ounces sharp Cheddar
cheese, shredded
1/4 teaspoon thyme
1/4 teaspoon basil

1/4 teaspoon marjoram
18 eggs, hard-cooked, thinly
sliced
1 pound bacon, crisp-cooked,
crumbled
1/4 cup chopped fresh parsley
Buttered bread crumbs

Heat the butter in a saucepan until melted. Stir in the flour. Add the milk and cream, whisking constantly. Cook until sauce is smooth and thickened, stirring constantly. Stir in the cheese, thyme, basil and marjoram. Cook until cheese is melted, stirring constantly. Layer the eggs, bacon, parsley and cheese sauce 1/3 at a time in a baking dish. Sprinkle with buttered bread crumbs. Bake at 350 degrees for 30 minutes.

Yield: 10 servings

SPICY EGG CASSEROLE

1 pound sausage
6 eggs
1/2 cup flour
1 teaspoon baking powder
1 cup milk
3 ounces cream cheese,
cut into small pieces
1 cup small curd cottage cheese
10 ounces Monterey Jack
cheese, shredded

6 ounces mild Cheddar cheese,
shredded
1/8 teaspoon salt
1 bunch green onions, chopped
2 (6-ounce) cans sliced mushrooms, drained
2 tablespoons butter
Paprika

Brown the sausage in a skillet, stirring until crumbly; drain. Beat the eggs with a whisk in a large bowl. Add the flour, baking powder and milk and mix well. Stir in the sausage and the next 7 ingredients. Spoon into a buttered 9×13-inch baking dish. Dot with butter. Sprinkle with the paprika. Chill, covered, for 8 to 12 hours. Bring to room temperature. Bake at 350 degrees for 45 minutes.

Yield: 10 to 12 servings

BROCCOLI QUICHE

2 cups finely chopped broccoli
1/2 cup chopped green bell pepper
1/3 cup chopped onion
1 cup shredded Colby cheese
1 cup milk
1/2 cup biscuit mix
3 eggs
1/4 teaspoon salt
1/4 teaspoon pepper

Bring a small amount of water to a boil in a saucepan. Add the broccoli. Cook for 10 minutes; drain. Arrange the broccoli evenly in a greased 9-inch pie plate. Sprinkle the bell pepper, onion and cheese over the broccoli. Combine the milk, biscuit mix, eggs, salt and pepper in a bowl and mix until smooth. Pour over the layers. Bake at 375 degrees for 25 minutes or until set. Let stand for 5 minutes.

Yield: 6 servings

QUICHE LORRAINE

8 slices peppered bacon, crisp-cooked
1 unbaked pie shell
3 ounces Swiss cheese, shredded
3 eggs, beaten
1/2 teaspoon dry mustard
1/2 cup milk
1/2 teaspoon salt
1/4 teaspoon pepper
1 cup heavy cream

Crumble the bacon into the pie shell. Sprinkle the cheese over the bacon. Combine the eggs, dry mustard, milk, salt, pepper and cream in a bowl and mix well. Pour over the cheese. Bake at 375 degrees for 35 to 45 minutes.

Yield: 6 servings

Soups and Salads

PETIT JEAN STATE PARK

The River Valley area of the state, carved by the Arkansas River, is home to three spectacular peaks—Mount Magazine, Mount Nebo, and Petit Jean Mountain. Atop Petit Jean you'll find the flagship of the state park system that proudly proclaims its Civilian Conservation Corps heritage with 60-year-old housekeeping cabins and the recently renovated Mather Lodge. Cedar Falls, the park's trademark waterfall, is a well-known attraction at Petit Jean.

ASPARAGUS LEMON SOUP

1 pound fresh asparagus, chopped
1 cup chopped celery
3 cups chicken broth
1/2 teaspoon grated lemon zest
2 tablespoons fresh lemon juice
Pinch of white pepper
1/2 cup heavy cream

Combine the asparagus, celery and chicken broth in a saucepan. Bring to a boil. Reduce the heat to low. Cook for 10 minutes. Let stand until cool. Purée in a blender or food processor. Stir in the lemon zest, lemon juice, white pepper and cream. Return to the saucepan. Cook until heated through; do not boil. Serve warm or cold.

Yield: 5 servings

AVOCADO DILL SOUP

1 (10-ounce) can chicken broth, chilled
1 chilled avocado, chopped
1/8 teaspoon lemon juice
1/4 cup half-and-half
1 tablespoon dry sherry
Dillweed for garnish

Combine the chicken broth, avocado, lemon juice, half-and-half and sherry in a food processor container. Process until smooth. Chill for 1 hour. Ladle into soup bowls. Garnish with dillweed.

Yield: 4 servings

BUTTERNUT SQUASH SOUP WITH SCALLION CREAM

2 (2-pound) butternut squash, peeled, cut into 2-inch pieces
1/4 cup (1/2 stick) unsalted butter, melted
Pinch of salt
Pinch of freshly ground pepper
1/4 cup (1/2 stick) unsalted butter
1 onion, coarsely chopped
2 celery ribs, cut into 1-inch pieces
1 leek, white and tender green portions only, coarsely chopped
1 large carrot, cut into 1-inch pieces
1 tablespoon finely chopped fresh gingerroot
1 tablespoon thyme leaves
8 cups chicken or vegetable stock
Salt and freshly ground pepper to taste
1/2 cup cold whipping cream
2 scallions, minced
2 chives, chopped

Toss the squash with the melted butter, pinch of salt and pinch of pepper in a large roasting pan. Arrange the squash evenly over the bottom of the pan. Bake at 375 degrees for 40 minutes or until the squash is tender, stirring occasionally.

Heat the butter in a large saucepan until melted. Add the onion, celery, leek and carrot. Cook over medium heat for 8 minutes or just until vegetables are tender, stirring occasionally. Stir in the gingerroot, thyme and baked squash. Add the stock. Bring to a boil over high heat. Reduce the heat to medium-low. Simmer, partially covered, for 20 minutes or until vegetables are very tender. Purée the soup in a blender in batches. Return to the saucepan. Season with salt and pepper. Cook until heated through.

Whip the cream in a mixing bowl until soft peaks form. Add the scallions and a pinch of salt. Whip until stiff peaks form. Ladle the soup into soup bowls. Garnish with a dollop of the scallion cream. Sprinkle with the chives. Serve immediately.

Note: You may substitute canned low-sodium chicken broth for the chicken stock.

Yield: 6 to 8 servings

BROCCOLI CHEESE SOUP

1 (10-ounce) package frozen chopped broccoli
1/4 cup chopped onion
1 tablespoon butter
16 ounces Velveeta, cubed
1 1/2 cups milk
Dash of pepper
Dash of garlic powder

Cook the broccoli using the package directions. Cook the onion in the butter in a skillet until tender. Spoon into a microwave-safe bowl. Add the broccoli, Velveeta, milk, pepper and garlic powder and stir to combine. Microwave, covered, on High for 3 minutes, stirring occasionally. Microwave until Velveeta is melted and mixture is hot and bubbly, stirring every 2 minutes. Let stand for 2 minutes. Ladle into soup bowls.

Yield: 4 to 6 servings

STUFFED SPUD SOUP

1/2 cup chopped green onions
1/2 cup (1 stick) butter
2 pounds frozen shredded hash brown potatoes, thawed
Salt and pepper to taste
1 (10-ounce) can cream of chicken soup
4 to 6 cups milk
1 cup shredded Cheddar cheese
Shredded Cheddar cheese for garnish

Sauté the green onions in the butter in a small skillet. Spoon into a large microwave-safe bowl. Add the potatoes, salt, pepper, soup and enough milk to make of the desired consistency. Microwave, covered, on High for 5 to 6 minutes. Stir in 1 cup cheese. Microwave until mixture boils, stirring every 2 minutes. Ladle into soup bowls. Garnish with additional cheese.

Yield: 8 to 10 servings

TOMATO GINGER SOUP

2¹/2 ounces fresh gingerroot, sliced
1 onion, coarsely chopped
2 pounds plum tomatoes, peeled, seeded, coarsely chopped
¹/4 cup (¹/2 stick) unsalted butter
1¹/4 cups chicken stock
1 tablespoon (or more) sugar
Salt to taste
Freshly ground white pepper to taste
³/4 cup heavy cream
2 egg yolks
Watercress leaves for garnish

Drop the gingerroot slices through the feed tube of a food processor while it is running. Process until minced. Add the onion and process until smooth. Spoon into a bowl. Place the tomatoes in the food processor container and purée.

Heat the butter in a large heavy saucepan over medium heat until melted. Add the gingerroot-onion mixture. Cook for 5 minutes or until the mixture begins to brown, stirring frequently. Add the tomato purée, chicken stock, sugar, salt and white pepper. Bring to a boil, stirring occasionally. Stir in the cream. Reduce the heat to low. Simmer for 30 minutes, stirring occasionally. Add additional sugar if desired.

Whisk the egg yolks in a small bowl. Stir a small amount of the hot tomato mixture into the beaten egg yolks. Stir the egg yolks into the hot tomato mixture. Cook over medium-low heat for 2 minutes or until the soup thickens; do not boil. Strain through a fine sieve into a separate saucepan. Cook until heated through. Ladle into 4 heated soup bowls. Garnish with watercress leaves.

Yield: 4 servings

ICY SPICY NEW MEXICAN SOUP

1 (35-ounce) can Italian tomatoes
1 tablespoon olive oil
1/2 cup chopped onion
1 teaspoon minced garlic
1 (4-ounce) can chopped green
chiles, drained
3 tablespoons flour
3 cups chicken broth
1 chicken bouillon cube
1/4 teaspoon cumin
1/4 teaspoon coriander
1/4 teaspoon salt
1/4 teaspoon pepper
1 teaspoon sugar
1/2 cup sour cream

Process the tomatoes in a blender for 30 seconds or until puréed. Heat the olive oil in a large saucepan over medium heat. Add the onion, garlic and green chiles. Cook for 3 minutes, stirring frequently. Add the flour. Cook for 1 minute, stirring constantly. Stir in the puréed tomatoes and chicken broth gradually. Add the bouillon cube, cumin, coriander, salt and pepper. Reduce the heat to low.

Simmer for 20 minutes, stirring frequetly. Remove from the heat. Stir in the sugar. Chill, covered, for 3 hours or longer. Stir in the sour cream. Chill for 2 to 4 hours.

Yield: 6 to 8 servings

HOMEMADE CHILI

1 pound bacon slices
2 yellow onions, chopped
1/4 cup olive oil
2 pounds breakfast sausage
2 pounds ground beef
2 1/4 teaspoons pepper
1 (12-ounce) can tomato paste
4 1/2 teaspoons minced garlic
1 1/2 ounces cumin
2 ounces chili powder
1/4 cup Dijon mustard
2 tablespoons salt
2 tablespoons basil
2 tablespoons oregano
2 (15-ounce) cans Italian plum tomatoes, drained
1/4 cup red wine
2 tablespoons lemon juice
2 tablespoons fresh dill
2 tablespoons chopped fresh parsley
1 cup (about) water

Cook the bacon in a skillet until crisp. Place on paper towels to drain. Sauté the onions in the olive oil in a large soup kettle. Add the sausage and ground beef. Cook until ground beef and sausage are brown and crumbly, stirring constantly; drain. Crumble the bacon into the ground beef mixture. Reduce the heat. Add the pepper, tomato paste, garlic, cumin, chili powder, mustard, salt, basil and oregano and mix well.

Add the tomatoes, wine, lemon juice, dill, parsley and enough water to make of the desired consistency and mix well. Simmer for 15 minutes. Adjust the seasonings. Simmer for 1 hour. Ladle into soup bowls. You may add beans or 1/4 cup jalapeño chile juice if desired.

Yield: 20 to 25 servings

CHICKEN CHILI

2 tablespoons canola oil
1 onion, chopped
2 large garlic cloves, minced
1 pound boneless skinless chicken breasts, cut into strips
4 teaspoons pure chili powder
1 tablespoon cumin
2 teaspoons oregano
3 cups chicken broth

1¹/2 cups canned chopped tomatoes
2 jalapeño chiles, chopped
Salt and freshly ground pepper
1 (15-ounce) can pinto or red beans, rinsed, drained
1 (15-ounce) can black beans, drained, rinsed
1/3 cup chopped fresh cilantro for garnish (optional)

Heat the canola oil in a large saucepan. Add the onion and garlic. Cook over medium-low heat just until tender. Add the chicken. Cook over medium heat for 3 minutes or until chicken is cooked through. Stir in the chili powder, cumin and oregano. Add the broth, tomatoes and jalapeño chiles. Season with salt and pepper. Cover and bring to a boil. Reduce the heat to low. Simmer for 15 minutes. Stir in the beans. Simmer, uncovered, over medium-low heat for 15 minutes or until the chili is thickened. Ladle into soup bowls. Garnish with cilantro.

Yield: 8 to 12 servings

BEAN STEW

6 bacon slices
3 garlic cloves, finely chopped
4 large onions, thinly sliced
3/4 cup packed brown sugar
1/4 cup vinegar
1 teaspoon dry mustard

1 (14-ounce) can kidney beans, drained
1 (14-ounce) can lima beans, drained
1 (31-ounce) can pork and beans

Cook the bacon in a skillet until crisp; drain on paper towels, reserving drippings in the skillet. Cool and finely chop. Add the garlic and onions to the bacon drippings. Cook until tender. Add the brown sugar, vinegar and dry mustard and mix well. Simmer for 10 minutes. Stir in the bacon pieces. Place the beans in a bowl, add the onion mixture and stir to combine. Spoon into a baking dish. Pour the sauce over the beans. Bake at 375 degrees for 45 to 60 minutes or until beans are tender.

Yield: 6 to 10 servings

OYSTER STEW

1 pint oysters
1/4 cup (1/2 stick) butter
1 teaspoon Worcestershire
sauce
1/2 teaspoon salt

Dash of cayenne pepper
4 cups warm half-and-half
Butter
Paprika

Combine the oysters, butter, Worcestershire sauce, salt and cayenne pepper in a saucepan. Cook until the edges of the oysters curl. Pour in the warm half-and-half. Ladle into individual bowls. Place a pat of butter on the stew. Sprinkle with paprika.

Yield: 4 servings

SHRIMP GUMBO

6 beef bouillon cubes
4 cups boiling water
3/4 cup chopped celery
1/2 cup chopped onion
2 teaspoons chopped garlic
1/3 cup olive oil
1 (16-ounce) can stewed tomatoes
2 (10-ounce) packages frozen gumbo vegetables

4 teaspoons salt
1 teaspoon pepper
1/2 teaspoon thyme
2 bay leaves
1 (16-ounce) can vegetable juice cocktail
2 cups rice
6 to 7 cups peeled fresh shrimp

Dissolve the bouillon cubes in the boiling water in a large saucepan. Add the celery, onion, garlic, olive oil, tomatoes, vegetables, salt, pepper, thyme, bay leaves and vegetable juice cocktail and mix well. Bring to a boil. Simmer for 20 minutes; remove bay leaves. Cook the rice using the package directions. Add the shrimp to the gumbo mixture. Simmer for 15 minutes. Spoon the rice into individual serving bowls. Spoon the gumbo over the rice.

Yield: 8 to 10 servings

LAYERED SALADS

LAYERED SALAD

1 pound fresh spinach, torn
1 head iceberg lettuce, torn
6 hard-cooked eggs, sliced
1 pound bacon, crisp-cooked, crumbled, or 1 (2-ounce) can bacon bits
1 (8-ounce) can sliced water chestnuts, drained
1 (10-ounce) package frozen English peas, thawed
1 cup mayonnaise or mayonnaise-type salad dressing
1/2 cup sour cream
1/2 envelope buttermilk-recipe salad dressing mix

Layer the spinach, lettuce, eggs, bacon, water chestnuts and peas in a large salad bowl. Combine the mayonnaise, sour cream and dressing mix in a bowl and mix well. Spread over the layers, sealing to the edge of the bowl. Chill, tightly covered, for 3 hours or longer. May sprinkle additional peas over the top.

Yield: 10 to 12 servings

CHEESY LAYERED SALAD

1 head lettuce, chopped
1/2 cup chopped bell pepper
1 red onion, chopped
1/2 cup chopped celery
1 (10-ounce) package frozen green peas, thawed
2 cups mayonnaise
2 tablespoons sugar
4 ounces Cheddar cheese, shredded
8 bacon slices, crisp-cooked, crumbled

Layer the lettuce, bell pepper, onion, celery and peas in a 9×13-inch dish or a large salad bowl. Combine the mayonnaise and sugar in a bowl and mix well. Spread over the layers, sealing to the edges. Sprinkle the cheese and bacon over the top. Chill, covered, for 8 hours or longer.

Yield: 10 to 12 servings

BROCCOLI SALAD

1 bunch broccoli
1 small purple onion, chopped
1/2 cup white raisins
1/2 cup sunflower seed kernels
8 ounces bacon, crisp-cooked, crumbled
Sweet and Sour Dressing

Separate the broccoli into florets. Combine the florets, onion, raisins and sunflower seed kernels in a salad bowl and mix well. Add the bacon and Sweet and Sour Dressing and toss to combine. Chill for 1 hour.

Yield: 4 to 6 servings

SWEET AND SOUR DRESSING

1/4 cup white vinegar
1/4 cup sugar
1 cup mayonnaise

Combine the vinegar, sugar and mayonnaise in a bowl and mix well. Chill, covered, until ready to use.

BROCCOLI AND CAULIFLOWER SALAD

2 cups chopped fresh broccoli, mostly florets
2 cups cauliflower florets
1/2 cup finely chopped red onion
1 bell pepper, chopped
Sour Cream Dressing

Combine the broccoli, cauliflower, onion and bell pepper in a salad bowl and toss to combine. Pour Sour Cream Dressing over the salad and mix well. Chill, covered, until ready to serve.

Yield: 4 servings

SOUR CREAM DRESSING

1/2 cup plus 2 tablespoons mayonnaise
1/4 cup (scant) sugar
1/2 cup plus 2 tablespoons sour cream
1/4 teaspoon salt

Combine the mayonnaise, sugar, sour cream and salt in a bowl and mix well.

SHOE PEG CORN SALAD

1 (11-ounce) can Shoe Peg corn, drained
1 (16-ounce) can French-style green beans, drained
1 (8-ounce) can small early sweet peas, drained
1 (2-ounce) jar pimentos, drained
1 small onion, chopped
Balsamic Vinegar and Oil Dressing

Combine the corn, green beans, peas, pimentos and onion in a salad bowl and mix well. Pour Balsamic Vinegar and Oil Dressing over the vegetables. Chill, covered, for 8 to 12 hours.

Yield: 4 servings

BALSAMIC VINEGAR AND OIL DRESSING

2/3 cup balsamic vinegar
1/3 cup vegetable oil
3/4 cup sugar
1 teaspoon salt
1/4 teaspoon pepper

Combine the vinegar, oil, sugar, salt and pepper in a saucepan. Cook until the sugar dissolves, stirring frequently. Let stand until cool.

BROCCOLI COLESLAW

2 (3-ounce) packages beef-flavor ramen noodles
1 (1-pound) package broccoli slaw
1 bunch green onions, chopped
Slaw Dressing
1 cup sunflower seed kernels
1 cup sliced almonds, toasted

Crumble the noodles. Reserve the seasoning packets for another use. Combine the noodles, broccoli slaw and green onions in a salad bowl and mix well. Pour Slaw Dressing over the mixture. Chill, covered, for 4 hours. Stir in the sunflower seed kernels and almonds. Serve immediately.

Yield: 4 to 6 servings

SLAW DRESSING

1/2 cup vegetable or light olive oil
1/3 cup vinegar
1/2 cup sugar

Combine the oil, vinegar and sugar in a microwave-safe bowl. Microwave until heated through.

SPECIAL SLAW

1/4 cup (1/2 stick) margarine
2 (3-ounce) packages chicken-flavor ramen noodles
1/4 cup slivered almonds, toasted
2 tablespoons sesame seeds
1 head cabbage, shredded
Oriental Dressing

Heat the margarine in a skillet until melted. Crush the noodles and add them to the skillet. Cook until brown, stirring frequently. Stir in the seasoning packets, almonds and sesame seeds and mix well. Spoon onto paper towels to cool. Combine the cooled noodle mixture, cabbage and Oriental Dressing in a bowl and toss to combine.

Yield: 8 to 12 servings

ORIENTAL DRESSING

1/3 cup vegetable oil
1/3 cup sugar
1 tablespoon soy sauce
1/4 cup rice wine vinegar
1/4 cup sesame oil

Combine the vegetable oil, sugar, soy sauce, vinegar and sesame oil in a bowl and mix well.

CHERRY SALAD

1 (6-ounce) package cherry gelatin
2 cups boiling water
1 (8-ounce) can crushed pineapple
1 (21-ounce) can cherry pie filling
1 cup sour cream
3 ounces cream cheese, softened
1/2 cup sugar
Chopped nuts

Dissolve the gelatin in the boiling water in a bowl. Stir in the pineapple and pie filling. Pour into a ring mold. Chill, covered, until set. Combine the sour cream, cream cheese and sugar in a bowl and mix until smooth. Spread over the gelatin. Sprinkle the nuts over the top.

Yield: 8 to 12 servings

CRANBERRY FRUIT MOLD

1 (6-ounce) package cranberry gelatin
2 cups boiling water
1 1/2 cups cold ginger ale
2 cups green or red seedless grape halves
1 (11-ounce) can mandarin orange slices, drained

Dissolve the gelatin in the boiling water in a bowl. Stir in the ginger ale. Chill for 1 1/2 hours or until partially set. Fold in the grapes and orange sections. Spoon into a 5-cup mold. Chill, covered, for 4 hours or until firm. Unmold onto a serving plate.

Yield: 10 servings

PRETZEL SALAD

1 (6-ounce) package strawberry gelatin
2 cups hot water
2 cups unsalted pretzels, crushed
3/4 cup (1 1/2 sticks) butter, melted
1 1/4 cups sugar
8 ounces nondairy whipped topping
8 ounces cream cheese, softened
2 (10-ounce) packages frozen strawberries

Dissolve the gelatin in the hot water in a bowl. Chill in the refrigerator. Sprinkle the crushed pretzels evenly over the bottom of a 9×13-inch baking pan. Pour the butter over the pretzels. Sprinkle 1/4 cup of the sugar over the pretzels. Press the layers together. Bake at 400 degrees for 2 minutes. Cream the remaining 1 cup sugar, whipped topping and cream cheese together in a mixing bowl until smooth. Spread over the baked layer. Stir the strawberries into the gelatin. Spoon over the cream cheese layer. Chill, covered, until firm.

Yield: 15 servings

SWEETHEART SALAD

1 (14-ounce) can sweetened condensed milk
1 (21-ounce) can cherry pie filling
1 cup nuts, chopped
12 ounces nondairy whipped topping
1 (15-ounce) can crushed pineapple, drained
1/2 cup marshmallows
1/2 cup shredded coconut

Combine the condensed milk, pie filling, nuts, whipped topping, pineapple, marshmallows and coconut in a bowl and mix well. Chill, covered, for 8 to 12 hours.

Yield: 8 to 12 servings

RICE SALAD

2 cups rice, cooked
1 cup chopped sweet pickles
1 cup chopped dill pickles
1 cup chopped bell pepper
1 1/2 cups chopped hard-cooked eggs
1 cup chopped pimento-stuffed olives
1 cup mayonnaise-style salad dressing
3 or 4 tablespoons Durkee Salad Dressing
3 or 4 tablespoons mustard
Dash of cayenne pepper
Dash of olive oil
Dash of wine vinegar
Dash of Louisiana hot sauce

Combine the rice, pickles, bell pepper, eggs, olives, salad dressings, mustard, cayenne pepper, olive oil, vinegar and hot sauce in a salad bowl and mix well. Chill, covered, for 8 to 12 hours.

Yield: 6 to 8 servings

SPINACH RICE SALAD

1 cup Italian salad dressing
2 tablespoons soy sauce
1 teaspoon sugar
6 cups chilled prepared rice
4 cups thinly cut fresh spinach
1 1/3 cups sliced celery
1 cup thinly sliced green onions
1 cup crumbled crisp-cooked bacon

Combine the Italian dressing, soy sauce and sugar in a large salad bowl and mix well. Add the rice and mix well. Chill, covered, until ready to serve. Stir in the spinach, celery, green onions and bacon. Serve immediately.

Yield: 16 servings

CONFETTI PASTA SALAD

16 ounces pasta, cooked
2 (14-ounce) cans artichoke hearts, chopped
1 (6-ounce) can pitted black olives, chopped
2 tomatoes, chopped
1 large red onion, chopped
1 green bell pepper, chopped
1 yellow bell pepper, chopped
1 large cucumber, chopped
2 cups chopped fresh mushrooms
2 or 3 celery ribs, chopped
1 1/2 (24-ounce) bottles zesty Italian salad dressing
1 (3-ounce) jar Salad Supreme seasoning

Combine the pasta, artichoke hearts, olives, tomatoes, red onion, bell peppers, cucumber, mushrooms, celery, Italian dressing and Salad Supreme seasoning in a large salad bowl and mix well. Chill, covered, for 3 hours or longer.

Yield: 8 to 10 servings

CORN BREAD SALAD

2 (6-ounce) packages Mexican corn bread mix
2 cups mayonnaise-style salad dressing
1 (16-ounce) can whole kernel corn, drained
1 cup chopped celery
1 cup chopped green bell pepper
1 bunch green onions, chopped
2 cups chopped firm tomatoes
Chopped jalapeño chiles to taste

Prepare the corn bread mix using the package directions. Let stand until cool. Crumble into a large salad bowl. Add the salad dressing, corn, celery, bell pepper, green onions, tomatoes and jalapeño chiles and mix well. Refrigerate until chilled through.

Yield: 8 to 10 servings

WILD TUNA SALAD

1 (6-ounce) package Uncle Ben's Long Grain and Wild Rice
1 cup mayonnaise
1/2 cup sour cream
1/2 cup finely chopped celery
2 tablespoons finely chopped onion
1 (12-ounce) can white albacore tuna, drained
1 cup salted cashews
Lettuce leaves
Alfalfa sprouts for garnish

Prepare the rice using the package directions. Chill in the refrigerator. Combine the chilled rice, mayonnaise, sour cream, celery, onion and tuna in a bowl and mix well. Stir in the cashews. Place the lettuce leaves on individual plates. Place a spoonful of the salad on each leaf. Garnish with alfalfa sprouts. You may substitute chicken or shrimp for the tuna.

Yield: 8 servings

CURRIED CRANBERRY CHICKEN SALAD

1/2 teaspoon curry powder
3/4 cup mayonnaise
2 teaspoons lime juice
2 cups chopped cooked chicken
1 apple, cut into 1/2-inch pieces
3/4 cup craisins
1/2 cup thinly sliced celery
1/4 cup chopped pecans
2 tablespoons thinly sliced green onions

Combine the curry, mayonnaise and lime juice in a bowl and mix well. Add the chicken, apple, craisins, celery, pecans and green onions and mix well. Chill, covered, for up to 8 hours.

Yield: 5 servings

CHICKEN SPINACH SALAD

1/2 cup lime juice
1/2 teaspoon garlic powder
1 teaspoon salt
1/2 teaspoon pepper
4 boneless chicken breasts
2 tablespoons vegetable oil
1 pound spinach leaves, torn
1 pint fresh strawberries
2 ounces almonds, lightly toasted
Poppy Seed Dressing

Combine the lime juice, garlic powder, salt and pepper in a sealable plastic bag and mix well. Add the chicken and swirl to coat. Seal the bag. Chill for 8 to 12 hours; drain. Heat the oil in a large skillet. Add the chicken breasts. Cook, covered, over medium-low heat for 15 to 20 minutes or until cooked through. Let stand until cool. Cut the chicken into 1/2-inch pieces, discarding the skin and bones.

Combine the chicken, spinach, strawberries and almonds in a salad bowl and mix well. Pour Poppy Seed Dressing over the salad.

Yield: 4 servings

POPPY SEED DRESSING

1/4 cup vegetable oil
1/2 cup sugar
1 1/2 teaspoons Worcestershire sauce
1/4 teaspoon paprika
1/4 cup cider vinegar
1 tablespoon poppy seeds
2 tablespoons sesame seeds, lightly toasted

Combine the oil, sugar, Worcestershire sauce, paprika and vinegar in a blender container. Process on High for 30 seconds. Pour into a small container. Stir in the poppy seeds and sesame seeds. Chill until ready to use.

CHICKEN SALAD

3 cups chopped cooked chicken
3 tablespoons lemon juice
1 1/2 cups chopped celery
1 cup seedless grapes
1 cup almond slivers
1 teaspoon dry mustard
1 teaspoon salt
1/4 teaspoon pepper
1/4 cup half-and-half
1 cup mayonnaise
2 hard-cooked eggs, sliced

Combine the chicken, lemon juice and celery in a bowl and mix well. Chill, covered, for 6 to 12 hours. Add the grapes, almonds, dry mustard, salt, pepper, half-and-half and mayonnaise and mix well. Spoon into a serving bowl. Arrange the egg slices over the salad.

Yield: 2 to 4 servings

HOT CHICKEN SALAD

1 cup chopped cooked chicken
1 (8-ounce) can sliced water chestnuts
4 hard-cooked eggs, sliced
1 (10-ounce) can cream of chicken soup
1 tablespoon fresh lemon juice
1 cup mayonnaise
Crushed potato chips

Combine the chicken, water chestnuts, eggs, soup, lemon juice and mayonnaise in a bowl and mix well. Spoon into a 9X12-inch baking dish. Sprinkle the potato chips over the top. Bake at 425 degrees for 20 minutes.

Yield: 6 to 8 servings

Entrées

SOUTHWEST NEWTON COUNTY,
GLORY HOLE

Newton County, the least populated county of 75 in Arkansas, seems to have as much in the way of wildlife as human life. This view of the Glory Hole is just one of many breathtaking views in the area. From the secluded Ozark Mountains to the meandering Buffalo River, Newton County is a gorgeous place to watch the outdoors go by.

BEST BARBECUED BRISKET

1/4 cup Worcestershire sauce
1/2 teaspoon sage
1/2 cup sugar
1 teaspoon celery salt
1/2 teaspoon Tabasco sauce
1/2 cup ketchup
1 (4-pound) beef brisket
Salt and pepper to taste

Combine the Worcestershire sauce, sage, sugar, celery salt, Tabasco sauce and ketchup in a saucepan and mix well. Cook until sugar dissolves, stirring frequently. Spoon 1/8 of the sauce over the bottom of a roasting pan. Sprinkle the brisket liberally with salt and pepper. Place in the pan over the sauce. Pour 1/3 of the remaining sauce over the brisket. Bake, covered, at 275 degrees for 4 1/2 hours. Cut into thin slices. Serve with the remaining sauce.

Yield: 12 to 16 servings

PEKING ROAST

1 (2- to 3-pound) brisket
4 garlic cloves
1 to 2 cups prepared instant coffee
1/2 cup soy sauce

Place the brisket in a roasting pan. Make small slits in the brisket. Cut the garlic cloves into slivers. Place in the slits in the brisket. Pour the coffee over the brisket. Pour the soy sauce over the brisket. Bake, covered, at 325 degrees for 2 to 2 1/2 hours.

Yield: 6 to 12 servings

SLOW-COOKED BRISKET

1 (8- to 10-pound) untrimmed brisket
3 to 4 teaspoons Dale's steak seasoning
1/4 cup Worcestershire sauce
Salt to taste
Seasoned pepper to taste
2 teaspoons thyme
1 onion, thinly sliced

Place the brisket, fat side down, in a large roasting pan. Pierce the brisket in several places. Pour the steak seasoning over the brisket. Let stand for 20 minutes. Sprinkle with Worcestershire sauce. Sprinkle with the salt, seasoned pepper and thyme. Arrange the onion slices over the brisket. Cover the pan with heavy-duty foil. Place the top on the roasting pan. Bake at 275 degrees for 6 hours; do not open the roaster. Let stand for 15 minutes. Cut the brisket cross grain into slices. Serve with barbeque sauce. You may add barbeque rub if desired.

Yield: 24 to 30 servings

FRENCH DIP SANDWICHES

1 (4-pound) arm or rump roast
Worcestershire sauce to taste
Garlic salt to taste
Oregano to taste
Pepper to taste
Basil to taste
1 (10-ounce) can beef broth
1 cup water
6 to 8 French rolls

Place the roast in a roasting pan. Pour the Worcestershire sauce over the roast. Sprinkle with the garlic salt, oregano, pepper and basil. Bake, covered, at 400 degrees for 15 minutes. Reduce the heat to 300 degrees. Pour the broth and water around the roast. Bake, covered, for 2 to 4 hours or until tender. Let stand for 10 minutes. Cut into thin slices. Layer the slices in the French rolls.

Yield: 6 to 8 servings

BEEF STROGANOFF

1/3 cup flour
1 (2-pound) 1/2-inch-thick round steak
1/4 cup (1/2 stick) butter
3/4 cup water
1 (4-ounce) can mushrooms
1 onion, chopped
1/2 teaspoon Worcestershire sauce
2 teaspoons salt
1/4 teaspoon pepper
2 cups sour cream

Pound the flour into the steak. Cut into strips 1/2 inch wide and 2 inches long. Heat the butter in a skillet until melted. Add the steak strips. Cook until brown on both sides. Stir in the water, mushrooms, onion, Worcestershire sauce, salt and pepper. Cook over low heat for 25 minutes, stirring occasionally. Stir in the sour cream. Serve over hot cooked rice or pasta.

Yield: 6 to 8 servings

NEW ORLEANS GRILLADES

1 (1/4-inch-thick) beef round steak, sliced
2 tablespoons (or more) vegetable oil
4 1/2 teaspoons flour
1 large onion, chopped
1 green bell pepper, chopped
2 garlic cloves, pressed
1 (14-ounce) can whole tomatoes, chopped
1 (10-ounce) can beef broth
1 1/2 teaspoons salt
1/4 to 1/2 teaspoon pepper
1 tablespoon Worcestershire sauce
1 tablespoon chopped parsley
1 or 2 large bay leaves

Cut the steak slices into twelve to twenty-four 2-inch rectangles. Heat the oil in a skillet. Add the steak pieces. Cook until brown on both sides. Remove from the pan. Add the flour to the drippings. Cook until slightly brown, stirring constantly and adding additional oil if needed. Add the onion, bell pepper and garlic. Cook until the vegetables are tender. Add the tomatoes, broth, salt, pepper, Worcestershire sauce, parsley and bay leaves. Stir until flour is dissolved, scraping the browned bits from the bottom of the skillet.

Add the steak pieces to the tomato mixture. Simmer over low heat for 1 hour. Remove bay leaves. Serve with rice, noodles or grits.

Yield: 4 to 6 servings

SOUTH-OF-THE-BORDER CASSEROLE

1 (9-ounce) package nacho
cheese tortilla chips
2 to 3 pounds ground beef
1 onion, chopped
1 (10-ounce) can cream of
mushroom soup

1 (10-ounce) can cream of
chicken soup
1 (12-ounce) can evaporated
milk
Chili powder to taste
8 slices American cheese

Sprinkle the chips over the bottom of a 9×13-inch baking dish. Brown the ground beef with the onion in a skillet, stirring until the ground beef is crumbly; drain. Add the soups, milk and chili powder and mix well. Spoon over the chips. Arrange the cheese slices over the top. Bake at 350 degrees for 15 minutes or until the cheese melts.

Yield: 6 to 12 servings

SOUTHWEST BEEF BAKE

2 tablespoons vegetable oil
1 1/2 pounds ground beef
or turkey
1 (15-ounce) can black beans,
drained
1 (14-ounce) can corn, drained
1 onion, chopped

1 cup sour cream
1 cup mild salsa
3 cups crushed tortilla chips
8 ounces Cheddar cheese,
shredded
1 tomato, chopped

Heat the oil in a skillet. Brown the ground beef in the hot oil, stirring until crumbly; drain. Combine the ground beef with the beans, corn, onion, sour cream and salsa in a bowl and mix well. Spoon enough of the beef mixture over the bottom of a 2-quart baking dish to cover the bottom. Layer the chips, cheese and remaining beef mixture half at a time over the beef mixture. Sprinkle the tomato over the top. Bake at 425 degrees for 10 to 12 minutes or until cheese is melted. You may substitute chopped cooked chicken breasts for the ground beef.

Yield: 4 to 6 servings

STUFFED GRAPE LEAVES

1 pound ground beef or lamb
1 cup rice
Salt and pepper to taste
Cinnamon to taste
1 (16-ounce) jar grape leaves, or 50 fresh tender grape leaves
1/4 cup lemon juice
1 garlic head (optional)

Combine the ground beef, rice, salt, pepper and cinnamon in a bowl and mix well. Place 1/2 to 1 teaspoon of the mixture on each grape leaf, depending upon the size of the leaf. Fold the sides in toward the center and roll up. Repeat with the remaining ingredients.

Place the rolls, seam side down, close to each other in a 3-quart saucepan. Pour the lemon juice over the rolls. Place a small plate over the rolls. Add enough water to cover up to the plate with water. Place the head of garlic on the plate. Bring to a boil. Reduce the heat to low.

Cook, covered, for 1 hour. You may place pieces of lamb bone in the saucepan if ground beef is used.

Yield: 8 servings

TACO PIE

1½ pounds ground beef
1 onion, chopped
1 bell pepper, chopped
1 envelope taco seasoning mix
1 (10-ounce) can tomato soup

1 (16-ounce) can green beans
1 (16-ounce) can whole
  kernel corn
1 (6-ounce) package corn
  bread mix

Brown the ground beef with the onion and bell pepper in a skillet, stirring until ground beef is crumbly; drain. Stir the taco seasoning mix and tomato soup into the ground beef mixture. Add the green beans and corn and mix well. Spoon into a 9×12-inch baking dish. Prepare the corn bread batter using the package directions. Spread over the ground beef mixture. Bake at 350 degrees for 30 to 40 minutes or until heated through and corn bread is done.

Yield: 6 to 8 servings

TALARINI

1 pound ground beef
3 tablespoons olive oil
1 garlic clove, minced
1 large onion, chopped
1 green bell pepper, chopped
1 (14-ounce) can stewed
  tomatoes

1 (16-ounce) can whole
  kernel corn
8 ounces American cheese, diced
1 (4-ounce) can sliced black
  olives
1 (12-ounce) package wide egg
  noodles

Brown the ground beef in the olive oil in a skillet, stirring until crumbly; drain. Stir in the garlic, onion and bell pepper. Sauté until vegetables are tender. Add the tomatoes and corn. Cook until heated through. Stir in the cheese and olives.

Cook the noodles using the package directions; drain. Stir into the ground beef mixture. Spoon into a buttered baking dish. Bake at 350 degrees for 1 hour.

Yield: 4 to 6 servings

CROWN OF LAMB WITH TRUFFLE MUSTARD SAUCE

1 rack of lamb, split, trimmed
Salt to taste
Freshly ground pepper to taste
3 tablespoons vegetable oil
2 onions, coarsely chopped
1 carrot, coarsely chopped
1 celery rib, coarsely chopped
1 garlic head, cut into halves
3 bay leaves
1/4 cup tomato paste
4 sprigs rosemary

4 sprigs thyme
1 cup chicken or lamb stock
1 cup red wine
1 tablespoon butter
2 cups Cream Spinach
(page 130)
Juice of 1 lemon, strained
1 egg yolk
3 tablespoons Dijon mustard
1/2 cup truffle oil
1 teaspoon chopped truffles

Tie the lamb rack together using butcher twine. Season with salt and pepper. Pour the oil into a roasting pan. Place the onions, carrot, celery, garlic and bay leaves in the pan and toss to coat with the oil. Stir in the tomato paste. Season with salt and pepper. Place the lamb on the vegetables. Place the rosemary and thyme on top of the lamb. Bake in a preheated 400-degree oven for 20 minutes. Add the stock and wine. Reduce the temperature to 350 degrees. Cook for 30 minutes for medium-rare or until done to taste. Remove from the oven. Set the lamb aside.

Strain the broth in the roasting pan. Place the strained broth in a saucepan. Bring to a simmer. Simmer for 5 minutes. Whisk in the butter. Season with salt and pepper.

Place the lemon juice into a nonreactive bowl. Whisk in the egg yolk. Whisk in the Dijon mustard until smooth. Pour the truffle oil in a slow steady stream into the lemon juice mixture, whisking constantly. Stir in the truffles. Season with pepper.

Spoon the Cream Spinach into the center of a serving plate. Place the lamb over the spinach. Drizzle the broth mixture and truffle mustard sauce over the lamb. Garnish with fresh herbs, bay leaves, rosemary or thyme.

Yield: 6 servings

CROWN ROAST WITH GRAVY

Salt and freshly ground pepper
1 (8- to 9-pound) crown roast of pork
5$\frac{1}{2}$ tablespoons olive oil
Grated zest of 1 orange
4 large garlic cloves, minced
2 tablespoons chopped fresh rosemary
3/4 cup dry white wine
1/2 cup fresh apple cider
1$\frac{1}{2}$ cups veal or chicken stock, preferably homemade
1 tablespoon butter, softened
2 tablespoons flour

Sprinkle salt and pepper over the roast. Brush 4 tablespoons of the olive oil over the roast. Combine the remaining 1$\frac{1}{2}$ tablespoons olive oil, orange zest, garlic and rosemary in a bowl and mix well. Spread evenly over the inside and outside of the roast. Place the roast in a heavy-duty roasting pan with a rack large enough to hold the roast without crowding the sides.

Bake in a preheated 425-degree oven on a rack in the lower third of the oven for 15 minutes. Reduce the heat to 375 degrees. Bake for 1$\frac{1}{2}$ hours or to 150 degrees on a meat thermometer, rotating the pan after 45 minutes. Place the roast on a cutting board. Let stand for 20 minutes.

Pour the pan juices into a measuring cup. Let stand for 5 to 10 minutes. Discard the fat and return the juices to the pan. Stir in the wine. Bring to a boil over medium-high heat, scraping the browned bits from the bottom of the pan. Boil for 5 to 7 minutes or until reduced by half. Stir in the apple cider and veal stock. Season with salt and pepper. Bring to a boil.

Combine the butter with the flour in a bowl and mix well. Add to the sauce. Cook for 4 to 5 minutes or until the gravy has thickened slightly, whisking constantly. Remove from the heat. Strain the gravy into a gravy boat. Place the roast on a serving platter and carve. Serve with the gravy.

Yield: 12 to 18 servings

COWBOY BEANS WITH SMOKED SAUSAGE

2 onions, coarsely chopped
1 green bell pepper, coarsely chopped
2 celery ribs, finely chopped
2 garlic cloves, minced
2 tablespoons olive oil
1 pound smoked sausage, cut into bite-size pieces
2 cups barbecue sauce
1/3 cup packed brown sugar
1/4 cup vinegar
2 tablespoons chopped chiles
1 tablespoon Worcestershire sauce
1 tablespoon mustard
2 tablespoons liquid smoke
1 tablespoon salt
$1^1/2$ teaspoons black pepper
3/8 teaspoon red pepper
1 (16-ounce) can pinto beans, drained
1 (16-ounce) can red beans, drained
1 (16-ounce) can red kidney beans, drained
1 (16-ounce) can Northern beans, drained
1 (16-ounce) can pork and beans, drained

Sauté the onions, bell pepper, celery and garlic in the olive oil in a Dutch oven until onions are partially cooked. Add the sausage. Sauté until onions are tender. Add the barbecue sauce, brown sugar, vinegar, chiles, Worcestershire sauce, mustard, liquid smoke, salt, black pepper, red pepper, pinto beans, red beans, kidney beans, Northern beans and pork and beans and mix well. Bake at 350 degrees for $1^1/4$ to $1^3/4$ hours.

Yield: 15 to 20 servings

PEPPERONI SPAGHETTI

16 ounces spaghetti
2 pounds ground beef or turkey
1 (3-ounce) package sliced pepperoni
1 large onion, chopped
2 (32-ounce) jars spaghetti sauce
8 ounces mozzarella cheese, shredded
8 ounces Cheddar cheese, shredded

Cook the spaghetti using the package directions; drain. Brown the ground beef with the pepperoni in a skillet, stirring until ground beef is crumbly. Remove to a bowl, reserving the drippings. Brown the onion in the drippings; drain. Stir the onion into the ground beef mixture. Layer the cooked spaghetti, ground beef mixture, spaghetti sauce, mozzarella cheese and Cheddar cheese half at a time in a 9×13-inch baking dish. Bake at 400 degrees for 20 minutes or until cheese is melted. You may substitute sautéed vegetables for the ground beef and pepperoni.

Yield: 8 to 10 servings

RED BEANS AND RICE

1 pound Cajun-style smoked sausage, sliced
3 tablespoons vegetable oil
2 (15-ounce) cans red beans, drained
2 cups water
1/4 cup Italian seasoning
2 tablespoons garlic powder
1 tablespoon sugar
Hot pepper sauce to taste
2 cups hot cooked rice

Brown the sausage in the oil in a skillet; drain. Place the sausage in a Dutch oven. Add the beans, water, Italian seasoning, garlic powder, sugar and hot pepper sauce and mix well. Bring to a boil. Reduce the heat. Simmer for 20 to 25 minutes, stirring occasionally. Serve over the rice.

Yield: 4 servings

BLONDIE'S CARBONARA

1 1/2 pounds bacon, chopped
3 tablespoons olive oil
1 large onion, chopped
1 large bell pepper, chopped
1/2 cup chopped mushrooms
3/4 cup (or more) dry
    white wine
Olive oil
Salt

1 (12-ounce) package fettuccini
2 eggs, beaten
1/2 cup (1 stick) butter, melted
3/4 cup grated Parmesan and
    Romano cheeses
1/3 cup chopped fresh parsley
1/2 cup olive oil
Freshly ground pepper

Cook the bacon in a skillet until light brown. Remove the bacon. Remove and discard the drippings, reserving a small amount. Add 3 tablespoons olive oil to the drippings in the skillet. Add the onion, bell pepper and mushrooms to the skillet and sauté until tender. Add the cooked bacon and wine, scraping the browned bits from the bottom of the skillet. Simmer for 5 to 10 minutes, adding additional wine as needed.

Bring a large pot of water to a boil. Add a small amount of olive oil and salt to the water. Return to a boil. Add the fettuccini and cook until al dente. Drain quickly and thoroughly. Return to the warm pot. Add the eggs, butter, cheeses, parsley, 1/2 cup olive oil and bacon mixture and mix well. Sprinkle generously with pepper.

Yield: 6 servings

PERFECT PORK CHOPS

4 pork chops, butterflied
Salt and pepper to taste

1 can cola
1/2 cup ketchup

Sprinkle the pork chops with salt and pepper. Place in a 9×13-inch baking dish. Combine the cola and ketchup in a bowl and mix well. Pour over the pork chops. Bake, covered, at 350 degrees for 1 hour.

Yield: 4 servings

CHICKEN FIESTA

1 (10-ounce) package corn chips
1 onion, chopped
Butter
1 (3-pound) chicken, cooked, cut into bite-size pieces
1 (10-ounce) can cream of mushroom soup
1 (5-ounce) can evaporated milk
1 (10-ounce) can tomatoes with green chiles
16 ounces Cheddar cheese, shredded

Crush the corn chips slightly. Sprinkle over the bottom of a 9X13-inch baking dish. Brown the onion in a small amount of butter in a skillet. Combine with the chicken, soup, milk and tomatoes and mix well. Spoon over the corn chips. Sprinkle the cheese over the top. Bake at 325 degrees for 30 minutes.

Yield: 10 to 12 servings

BALSAMIC MARINATED CHICKEN

1/4 cup balsamic vinegar
1/4 cup honey
1/4 cup olive oil
2 tablespoons fresh rosemary
1 teaspoon salt
3 pounds chicken breasts, thighs and legs

Combine the vinegar, honey, olive oil, rosemary and salt in a sealable plastic bag and mix well. Add the chicken, coating with the marinade. Seal the bag and marinate in the refrigerator for 2 hours, turning occasionally.

Drain the chicken, reserving the marinade. Place the chicken in a greased 9X13-inch baking dish. Pour the reserved marinade over the chicken. Bake at 375 degrees for 45 minutes or until cooked through, basting frequently. You may substitute boneless skinless chicken breasts for the chicken parts.

Yield: 4 servings

CHICKEN ARTICHOKE CASSEROLE

6 chicken breasts
1 1/2 teaspoons salt
1/2 teaspoon pepper
1/2 teaspoon paprika
1/4 cup (1/2 stick) butter
2 (6-ounce) jars marinated
artichoke hearts

2 tablespoons butter
4 ounces mushrooms, coarsely
chopped
2 tablespoons flour
3 tablespoons sherry
2/3 cup chicken broth

Sprinkle the chicken with the salt, pepper and paprika. Heat 1/4 cup butter in a skillet until melted. Add the chicken and brown on both sides. Place the chicken in a large baking dish, reserving the drippings in the skillet. Arrange the artichoke hearts around the chicken. Heat 2 tablespoons butter in the reserved drippings until melted. Add the mushrooms and cook until tender. Sprinkle the flour over the mushrooms. Stir in the sherry and broth. Cook for 5 minutes, stirring occasionally. Pour over the chicken and artichokes. Bake, covered, at 375 degrees for 40 minutes.

Yield: 6 servings

CHICKEN CROISSANTS

2 pounds chicken pieces
2 (16-ounce) cans cream of
chicken soup
1 (16-ounce) can cream of
mushroom soup

1/2 cup milk
Shredded cheese
2 packages croissant dough
Shredded cheese

Combine the chicken with enough water to cover in a saucepan. Bring to a boil. Reduce the heat. Simmer until cooked through; drain. Let stand until cool. Shred the chicken. Combine the soups and milk in a bowl and mix well. Combine the chicken with enough soup mixture to moisten in a bowl and mix well. Place a small amount of the chicken mixture and cheese in a croissant pastry. Roll to enclose the filling. Place in a baking dish. Repeat with the remaining ingredients. Pour the remaining soup mixture over the croissants. Sprinkle cheese over the top. Bake at 350 degrees for 25 minutes.

Yield: 6 to 8 servings

CHICKEN BREASTS VERONIQUE

CHICKEN BREASTS VERONIQUE

4 boneless skinless chicken
breasts
Salt
1 tablespoon (heaping) tarragon
1 tablespoon butter or
margarine
1 tablespoon orange marmalade
1/4 teaspoon tarragon, crumbled

1/4 cup dry white wine
1/4 cup heavy cream
1/2 teaspoon cornstarch
2 teaspoons water
3/4 cup seedless grapes
8 mushrooms, sliced (optional)
2 tablespoons butter (optional)
Parsley for garnish

Bring enough water to cover the chicken to a boil in a large saucepan. Add the chicken, a small amount of salt and 1 tablespoon tarragon. Simmer until chicken is partially cooked; drain. Heat 1 tablespoon butter in a skillet until melted. Add the chicken, marmalade, 1/4 teaspoon tarragon and wine. Simmer, covered, for 15 minutes or until chicken is cooked through. Place the chicken on a serving dish and keep warm. Add the cream to the pan juices. Bring to a boil. Combine the cornstarch and water in a small bowl. Stir into the cream mixture. Bring to a boil, stirring constantly. Stir in the grapes. Bring to a boil. Pour the sauce over the chicken. Sauté the mushrooms in 2 tablespoons butter in a skillet until tender. Spoon over the sauce. Garnish with parsley.

Yield: 4 servings

CHICKEN ENCHILADAS

16 ounces Velveeta cheese, cubed
1 (10-ounce) can tomatoes with
green chiles
4 boneless skinless chicken
breasts, cooked, chopped

Butter
1 (10-ounce) can enchilada sauce
Large flour tortillas
1 (10-ounce) can enchilada sauce

Heat the cheese and tomatoes in a saucepan until the cheese is melted, stirring frequently. Set aside. Brown the chicken in a small amount of butter in a skillet. Add 1 can of enchilada sauce. Simmer for 15 minutes. Spoon the chicken mixture and cheese mixture down the center of each tortilla. Roll to enclose the filling. Place, seam side down, in a baking dish. Pour 1 can of enchilada sauce and remaining cheese mixture over the enchiladas. Bake at 350 degrees for 15 minutes.

Yield: 6 to 8 servings

CHICKEN PASTA

3 tablespoons lemon juice

3 tablespoons soy sauce

2 garlic cloves

1 teaspoon basil

Freshly ground pepper

2 boneless skinless chicken breasts

2 tablespoons stir-fry sauce

1 tablespoon ginger soy sauce or regular soy sauce

1/4 cup white wine

1 onion, chopped

1 red bell pepper, sliced

1 yellow bell pepper, sliced

1 green bell pepper, sliced

2 teaspoons basil

1 pound mushrooms, sliced

1 (8-ounce) can tomato sauce

16 ounces angel hair pasta

Fresh cilantro for garnish

2 tomatoes, cut into wedges for garnish

1/4 cup grated Parmesan cheese for garnish

Combine the lemon juice, soy sauce, garlic, 1 teaspoon basil and pepper in a sealable plastic bag and mix well. Add the chicken, coating with the marinade. Marinate in the refrigerator; drain. Pound between sheets of waxed paper. Grill over hot coals for 5 minutes on each side. Let cool. Cut into 1 1/2-inch pieces.

Coat a wok with nonstick cooking spray. Combine the stir-fry sauce, soy sauce, wine, onion and bell peppers in the wok. Cook over medium heat for 10 minutes or until the onion is lightly browned, stirring frequently. Add 2 teaspoons basil, mushrooms and tomato sauce and mix well.

Cook the pasta using the package directions; drain. Combine the pasta, chicken and bell pepper mixture in a large bowl and toss to combine. Garnish with cilantro, tomato wedges and cheese.

Yield: 4 servings

CHICKEN PARMESAN

1 tablespoon extra-virgin olive oil
2 tablespoons chicken broth
1 small onion, finely chopped
2 garlic cloves, minced
1 cup crushed Italian tomatoes
1 teaspoon minced fresh oregano
1/8 teaspoon crushed red pepper flakes
1 tablespoon minced fresh basil
1/2 teaspoon salt
4 boneless skinless chicken breasts
1/4 cup flour
2 tablespoons extra-virgin olive oil
4 slices part-skim mozzarella cheese
Hot cooked pasta
Minced fresh basil

Bring 1 tablespoon olive oil and chicken broth to a boil in a saucepan over medium heat. Add the onion and cook for 3 minutes. Add the garlic and cook for 1 minute. Add the tomatoes, oregano, red pepper flakes, 1 tablespoon basil and salt and mix well. Cook for 5 minutes, stirring frequently.

Coat the chicken with the flour. Heat 2 tablespoons olive oil over medium heat in a skillet. Add the chicken and cook for 4 minutes. Turn and cook for 2 minutes. Place a slice of cheese over each chicken breast. Cook, covered, for 2 to 3 minutes or until cheese is melted.

Sprinkle the pasta with minced basil. Spoon the sauce over the pasta. Arrange the chicken over the sauce.

Yield: 4 servings

CHICKEN ROMANO

1/3 cup flour
1/2 teaspoon salt
1/4 teaspoon pepper
4 boneless skinless chicken breasts
2 tablespoons vegetable oil
1/4 cup minced onion
2 cups tomato juice
2 tablespoons grated Romano cheese
1 tablespoon sugar
1/2 teaspoon salt
1/2 teaspoon garlic powder
1/2 teaspoon oregano
1/4 teaspoon basil
1 teaspoon red wine vinegar
1 (4-ounce) can sliced mushrooms, drained
1 tablespoon minced parsley
1/2 cup grated Romano cheese
Hot cooked spaghetti

Combine the flour, salt and pepper in a shallow dish and mix well. Dredge the chicken in the flour mixture. Brown the chicken in the hot oil in a skillet. Remove and place on paper towels to drain. Discard the pan drippings, reserving 1 tablespoon.

Sauté the onion in the reserved drippings. Add the tomato juice, 2 tablespoons cheese, sugar, salt, garlic powder, oregano, basil, vinegar, mushrooms and parsley and mix well. Add the chicken. Simmer, covered, for 45 minutes or until chicken is tender. Sprinkle with 1/2 cup cheese. Serve over the spaghetti. You may substitute Parmesan cheese for the Romano cheese.

Yield: 6 servings

CHICKEN SPAGHETTI

4 boneless skinless chicken breasts
Lemon pepper to taste
1 (8-ounce) package spaghetti
1 onion, chopped
1 bell pepper, chopped
Butter
1 (10-ounce) can cream of mushroom soup
16 ounces mozzarella cheese, shredded

Sprinkle the chicken lightly with lemon pepper. Place in a saucepan with enough water to cover. Bring to a boil. Boil until cooked through. Drain, reserving the broth. Let chicken stand until cool. Shred the chicken. Cook the spaghetti using the package directions; drain. Sauté the onion and bell pepper in a small amount of butter in a skillet until tender. Heat the soup in a saucepan. Add enough of the reserved chicken broth to make a thin mixture.

Layer the spaghetti, onion mixture, cheese and soup in a 9X13-inch baking dish half at a time. Bake at 350 degrees for 5 to 10 minutes or until the cheese melts.

Yield: 6 to 8 servings

CHICKEN SUPERB

8 ounces dried chipped beef
8 boneless chicken breasts
8 bacon slices
2 cups sour cream
2 (10-ounce) cans cream of mushroom soup

Arrange the chipped beef over the bottom of a buttered shallow baking dish. Arrange the chicken over the chipped beef. Place a slice of bacon over each piece of chicken.

Combine the sour cream and soup in a bowl and mix well. Pour over the layers. Bake, covered, at 300 degrees for 2 hours. Remove the cover. Bake for 1 hour or until browned.

Yield: 8 servings

CREAMY CHICKEN PASTA WITH SPINACH AND TOMATOES

1 (9-ounce) package frozen chopped spinach, thawed
2 cups pasta, such as penne or ziti
4 boneless skinless chicken breasts
1 (10-ounce) can chicken broth
1 teaspoon chopped garlic
1 teaspoon salt
1 tablespoon pepper
8 ounces cream cheese
15 cherry tomatoes, cut into halves
1/2 cup grated Parmesan cheese

Drain the spinach, pressing out the excess moisture. Cook the pasta using the package directions; drain. Set aside and keep warm.

Cut the chicken into 1-inch pieces. Combine with half of the chicken broth in a large skillet. Cook for 5 to 7 minutes or until chicken is cooked through, turning frequently. Add the remaining chicken broth, garlic, salt, pepper, spinach and cream cheese. Cook for 3 to 5 minutes or until cream cheese is melted, stirring frequently. Add the tomatoes. Cook for 2 to 3 minutes or until tomatoes are tender, stirring frequently. Toss the chicken mixture with the pasta in a large bowl. Sprinkle with the Parmesan cheese.

Yield: 4 to 6 servings

CHICKEN TARRAGON

1/2 cup (1 stick) butter
8 chicken breasts
Salt and pepper to taste
1/2 teaspoon tarragon
1 cup sour cream
1/4 cup grated Parmesan cheese
2 cups mushrooms

Place the butter in a 9X13-inch baking dish. Heat in a 375-degree oven until melted. Remove from the oven. Dip the chicken in the butter and place in the pan. Sprinkle with salt, pepper and tarragon. Bake, covered, at 375 degrees for 50 minutes. Remove the chicken. Add the sour cream and cheese to the drippings and mix well. Stir in the mushrooms. Arrange the chicken over the mushroom mixture. Bake for 10 minutes.

Yield: 8 servings

LEMON CHICKEN

4 chicken breasts, cooked, chopped
1 (10-ounce) can cream of chicken soup
1 cup sour cream
1/2 cup lemon juice
1 sleeve butter crackers, crushed
1/2 cup (1 stick) margarine, melted
3 tablespoons poppy seeds

Sprinkle the chicken over the bottom of a greased 9X13-inch baking pan. Combine the soup, sour cream and lemon juice in a bowl and mix well. Pour over the chicken. Sprinkle the cracker crumbs over the layers. Drizzle the butter over the cracker crumbs. Sprinkle the poppy seeds over the top. Bake at 350 degrees for 30 to 45 minutes.

Yield: 4 servings

LEMON MUSTARD CHICKEN BREASTS

2 tablespoons minced fresh parsley
1 garlic clove, minced
1 teaspoon Dijon mustard
1/4 teaspoon red pepper flakes
1/2 teaspoon crushed fennel seeds
Juice of 1 lemon
4 boneless chicken breasts

Combine the parsley, garlic, Dijon mustard, red pepper flakes, fennel seeds and lemon juice in a sealable plastic bag and mix well. Add the chicken, coating with the marinade. Seal the bag and marinate for 15 minutes at room temperature; drain. Place chicken on a grill over hot coals. Grill for 5 minutes on each side or until cooked through.

Yield: 4 servings

POPPY SEED CHICKEN

6 large chicken breasts
Salt and pepper to taste
2 (10-ounce) cans cream of chicken soup
2 cups sour cream
40 butter crackers, crushed
2 tablespoons poppy seeds
1/2 cup (1 stick) margarine, melted

Combine the chicken, salt and pepper with enough water to cover the chicken in a saucepan. Bring to a boil. Boil until chicken is cooked through; drain. Let stand until cool. Cut into bite-size pieces. Arrange evenly in a 9x13-inch baking dish.

Combine the soup and sour cream in a bowl and mix well. Pour over the chicken. Combine the cracker crumbs and poppy seeds in a bowl and mix well. Sprinkle over the layers. Pour the margarine over the top. Bake at 350 degrees for 30 minutes or until bubbly.

Yield: 10 to 12 servings

SMOTHERED CHICKEN

5 chicken breasts
Salt to taste
Black pepper to taste
Red pepper to taste
Vegetable oil
1 pound Cajun sausage, sliced

1 onion, chopped
1 bell pepper, chopped
1/2 cup chopped celery
2 teaspoons garlic powder
2 cups water

Sprinkle the chicken with salt, black pepper and red pepper. Brown the chicken in a small amount of oil in a skillet. Remove from the skillet. Brown the sausage in the skillet. Remove the sausage from the skillet. Discard the drippings, reserving a small amount. Sauté the onion, bell pepper and celery in the reserved drippings in the skillet until tender. Add the browned chicken and sausage. Sprinkle with the garlic powder. Add the water gradually. Simmer, covered, for 30 to 40 minutes. Serve with rice.

Yield: 8 to 10 servings

CHICKEN FRIED RICE

1 tablespoon vegetable oil
1 egg, beaten
2 tablespoons vegetable oil
1 cup finely chopped chicken
1 onion, finely chopped
1 cup fresh bean sprouts
1/2 cup frozen peas
1/2 cup finely chopped celery

1/2 cup finely chopped water chestnuts
1/2 cup finely chopped bamboo shoots
1 cup sliced fresh mushrooms
4 cups cooked rice
Soya sauce to taste
Salt and pepper to taste

Heat 1 tablespoon oil in a wok. Add the egg. Fry into a thin sheet. Remove to a plate. Add 2 tablespoons oil and heat until smoking. Add the chicken and onion. Cook until chicken is cooked through and onion is tender. Add the bean sprouts, peas and celery. Cook, covered, for 2 minutes. Add the water chestnuts, bamboo shoots and mushrooms. Cook, covered, for 2 minutes. Add the rice, Soya sauce, salt and pepper. Reduce the heat to medium. Cook until rice has absorbed the sauce, stirring constantly. Turn the heat off. Cut the egg into small pieces and stir into the stir-fry mixture.

Yield: 4 to 6 servings

THREE-CHEESE CHICKEN BAKE

3 tablespoons butter or margarine
1/2 cup chopped onion
1/2 cup chopped green bell pepper
1 (10-ounce) can cream of chicken soup
1 (8-ounce) can sliced mushrooms, drained
1 (2-ounce) jar chopped pimentos, drained
1/2 teaspoon basil
1 (8-ounce) package noodles, cooked
3 cups chopped cooked chicken
2 cups ricotta or cottage cheese
2 cups shredded Cheddar cheese
1/2 cup grated Parmesan cheese
1/4 cup buttered bread crumbs

Heat the butter in a skillet until melted. Add the onion and bell pepper. Sauté until onion and bell pepper are tender. Remove from the heat. Add the soup, mushrooms, pimentos and basil and mix well.

Combine the noodles, chicken, ricotta cheese, Cheddar cheese and Parmesan cheese in a large bowl and mix well. Add the mushroom mixture and mix well. Spoon into a greased 9X13-inch baking pan.

Bake at 350 degrees for 40 to 45 minutes or until bubbly. Sprinkle the bread crumbs over the top. Bake for 15 minutes longer.

Yield: 12 to 15 servings

GRILLED MARINATED DUCK BREASTS

6 boneless duck breasts
2 tablespoons salt
2 cups Italian salad dressing
1 tablespoon Worcestershire sauce
6 bacon slices

Place the duck in a bowl. Add the salt and enough water to cover the duck. Let stand for 30 minutes; drain. Place the duck in a shallow dish. Combine the Italian dressing and Worcestershire sauce in a bowl and mix well. Pour over the duck. Marinate, in the refrigerator, for $1^1/2$ hours or longer, turning occasionally; drain. Wrap each duck breast with a slice of bacon, securing with wooden picks. Grill over medium coals until bacon and duck are cooked through.

Yield: 6 servings

WILD DUCK SUPREME

Wild duck meat, cut into 1-inch pieces
Vegetable oil
1 cup chopped celery
1 cup chopped green bell pepper
1 small onion, chopped
1 tablespoon Worcestershire sauce
$1/3$ cup dark corn syrup
1 to $1^1/2$ cups sauterne or white wine of choice
1 (4-ounce) can mushrooms
Salt and pepper to taste

Brown the duck in a small amount of oil in a skillet. Place the duck in a baking dish. Add the celery, bell pepper, onion, Worcestershire sauce, corn syrup, wine and mushrooms to the pan drippings and mix well. Cook until of the desired consistency. Season with salt and pepper. Pour over the duck. Bake at 300 to 350 degrees for 2 hours or until duck is tender, basting with the pan juices occasionally. Serve over rice.

Yield: Variable

SMOTHERED SOUTHERN QUAIL

1 cup flour
Salt to taste
Pepper to taste
2 tablespoons crushed rosemary
1¹/2 teaspoons garlic powder
2 tablespoons onion salt
8 quail, skinned
1/2 cup (or more) margarine or butter
1/2 cup water
1 (10-ounce) can cream of celery soup
1 (10-ounce) can cream of mushroom soup
1 tablespoon crushed rosemary
1 teaspoon garlic powder
1 teaspoon pepper
1 teaspoon celery salt
1 tablespoon parsley
1/2 cup white wine

Combine the flour, salt, pepper, 2 tablespoons rosemary, 1¹/2 teaspoons garlic powder and onion salt in a shallow dish and mix well. Dredge the quail in the flour mixture to coat well.

Heat the margarine in a large skillet until melted. Add the quail and brown on both sides. Pour in the water. Reduce the heat. Combine the soups, 1 tablespoon rosemary, 1 teaspoon garlic powder, 1 teaspoon pepper, celery salt, parsley and wine in a bowl and mix well. Pour over the quail. Simmer, covered, until quail are tender, adding additional margarine if needed. You may substitute pheasant, grouse or Cornish hens cut into pieces for the quail.

Yield: 4 servings

SALMON STEAKS WITH SAUCE

1/4 cup (1/2 stick) margarine, melted
1 tablespoon lemon juice
4 salmon steaks
Salt and pepper to taste
Mustard Dill Sauce or Caper Sauce

Combine the margarine and lemon juice in a bowl and mix well. Brush over 1 side of the salmon. Place on a greased grill rack, coated side down. Grill for 10 minutes per inch of thickness, turning once and brushing with the margarine mixture. Season with salt and pepper. Serve with Mustard Dill Sauce or Caper Sauce.

Yield: 4 servings

MUSTARD DILL SAUCE

1 cup mayonnaise
1/4 cup Dijon mustard
2 tablespoons lemon juice
1/4 teaspoon dillweed

Combine the mayonnaise, Dijon mustard, lemon juice and dillweed in a bowl and mix well. Chill, covered, until ready to serve.

CAPER SAUCE

2 tablespoons sour cream
2 tablespoons mayonnaise
1 teaspoon capers, drained
1/2 teaspoon white wine vinegar
1/4 teaspoon lemon pepper seasoning

Combine the sour cream, mayonnaise, capers, vinegar and lemon pepper seasoning in a bowl and mix well. Chill, covered, until ready to serve.

GLAZED TERIYAKI SALMON

4 (4- to 6-ounce) salmon fillets
1/3 cup orange juice
1/4 cup dry white wine
1 tablespoon grated fresh gingerroot
1 teaspoon lemon juice
1 garlic clove, minced
1/3 cup soy sauce
2 tablespoons vegetable oil
1 teaspoon dry mustard
Pinch of sugar
1/2 teaspoon freshly ground pepper

Place the salmon in a single layer in a shallow dish. Combine the orange juice, wine, gingerroot, lemon juice, garlic, soy sauce, oil, dry mustard, sugar and pepper in a bowl and mix well. Pour over the salmon. Marinate, covered, in the refrigerator, for 30 minutes, turning once.

Drain the salmon, reserving the marinade. Place the salmon in a single layer in a 9X13-inch baking pan. Bake at 450 degrees for 10 minutes or until salmon flakes easily. Remove from the oven and keep warm.

Bring the reserved marinade to a boil in a saucepan. Cook for 6 to 8 minutes or until reduced by half, stirring frequently. Place the salmon on a serving platter. Pour the sauce over the salmon.

Yield: 4 servings

ROASTED RED SNAPPER WITH GREEN OLIVES

4 red snapper fillets
2 garlic cloves, finely chopped
1/2 cup fresh parsley leaves
1/4 cup olive oil
1/4 cup white wine vinegar
Salt and pepper to taste
1 cup green olives, pitted, chopped
2 tablespoons chopped fresh parsley

Spray a baking pan just large enough to hold the snapper fillets with nonstick cooking spray. Rinse the fillets and pat dry. Place in the prepared pan. Sprinkle with garlic and parsley leaves. Drizzle with olive oil and vinegar. Sprinkle with salt and pepper. Sprinkle the olives over the top. Bake at 400 degrees for 25 minutes or until the flesh near the bone is just barely opaque, basting with the pan juices occasionally.

Plane the snapper on a serving platter. Pour the pan juices over the snapper. Sprinkle with chopped parsley. You may substitute pompano, sea bass or another white fish for the snapper.

Yield: 4 servings

TUNA WITH MANGO-GINGER-LIME MOJO

1 cup mango juice

1/2 teaspoon minced fresh gingerroot

2 mangoes, chopped

3 scallions, thinly sliced

1 red bell pepper, chopped

2 tablespoons minced dried mango

1 teaspoon minced crystallized ginger

1/4 cup lime juice

2 tablespoons minced fresh cilantro

1 serrano chile, minced

1/4 cup canola oil

Pinch of salt

Vegetable oil

Tuna steaks

Combine the mango juice and gingerroot in a saucepan. Bring to a boil. Boil until reduced by half. Remove from the heat. Let stand until completely cool. Add the chopped mango, scallions, bell pepper, dried mango, crystallized ginger, lime juice, cilantro, chile, canola oil and salt and mix well.

Brush a small amount of vegetable oil over the tuna steaks. Grill over hot coals for 2 to 3 minutes on each side for rare, 4 to 5 minutes on each side for medium rare and 6 to 7 minutes on each side for well-done. Place on a serving platter. Serve with the mojo.

Yield: Variable

CRABTOWN CRAB

1 pound crab meat

3/4 cup (1 1/2 sticks) butter or margarine

1/2 teaspoon salt

Pinch of black pepper

Pinch of cayenne pepper

Pinch of garlic powder

1 1/2 teaspoons lemon juice

1/4 cup (or more) dry sherry

Paprika for garnish

Trim the crab meat. Heat the butter in a skillet until melted. Add the salt, black pepper, cayenne pepper, garlic powder, lemon juice and sherry and mix well. Remove from the heat. Fold in the crab meat. Spoon the crab mixture into individual ramekins. Sprinkle the paprika over the top. Bake at 350 degrees for 10 to 15 minutes or until heated through.

Yield: 4 servings

EASTERN SHORE CRAB CAKES

1 pound fresh crab meat,
drained, flaked
1/2 to 3/4 cup mayonnaise
1/2 cup fine dry bread crumbs
1 egg, beaten
1 teaspoon mustard

3/4 to 1 teaspoon white
pepper
1/4 teaspoon parsley flakes
Pinch of salt
Vegetable oil for frying

Combine the crab meat, mayonnaise, bread crumbs, egg, mustard, white pepper, parsley and salt in a bowl and mix well. Shape into 10 patties. Heat the oil in a skillet. Fry the patties in the hot oil until golden brown on all sides. Place on paper towels to drain. You may serve these in a hamburger bun.

Yield: 5 servings

LOBSTER TAILS AND PASTA SALAD
WITH GARLIC SAUCE

4 (8-ounce) lobster tails, or
1 pound scallops
1/2 cup Asian-style marinade
or dressing
1 garlic head, caramelized
1 red bell pepper, chopped

2 green onions, chopped
2 cups chopped bok choy
greens
1 pound linguini, cooked,
chilled

Place the lobster tails in a shallow dish. Pour 1/4 cup of the marinade over the lobster. Marinate for 10 minutes. Drain, reserving the marinade. Grill over medium heat for 2 to 3 minutes, turning once. Brush with the reserved marinade. Grill over low heat for 5 minutes or until lobster meat is opaque. Separate the cloves from the garlic head. Stir-fry the bell pepper, green onions and bok choy in the remaining 1/4 cup marinade in a wok for 2 minutes. Stir in the garlic cloves.

Combine the linguini and vegetable mixture in a large bowl and toss to combine. Slice the lobster tails into 2-inch pieces. Add to the linguini mixture and toss to combine. You may substitute 2 teaspoons sesame oil, 1 tablespoon ginger, 2 tablespoons hoisin sauce and 1 tablespoon light soy sauce for the 1/2 cup Asian-style marinade.

Yield: 4 servings

SCALLOPS AND MUSHROOMS IN FOIL

8 ounces fresh scallops
8 ounces fresh mushrooms, sliced
1/4 cup (1/2 stick) margarine
2 tablespoons minced fresh parsley

Cut two 12-inch squares of heavy-duty foil. Place half of the scallops, mushrooms, margarine and parsley on each square. Double fold the foil and seal the ends. Grill on a grill rack or in the coals for 12 minutes or until scallops are tender.

Yield: 2 servings

EASY SHRIMP ALFREDO

5 tablespoons butter
2 teaspoons minced garlic
3 tablespoons flour
1/4 cup finely chopped fresh parsley
2 cups heavy cream
1 pound frozen peeled boiled medium shrimp with the tail on, thawed
1 tomato, chopped
Milk (optional)
1 cup grated Parmesan cheese
Hot cooked linguini or fettuccini

Heat the butter in a skillet until melted. Add the garlic and flour. Cook over medium heat until mixture starts to brown, stirring constantly. Set aside 1 tablespoon of the parsley. Stir the remaining parsley into the flour mixture. Cook for 1 minute. Add the cream, whisking constantly. Cook until mixture begins to thicken, stirring constantly.

Stir the shrimp and tomato into the cream mixture. Cook until of the desired consistency and shrimp are heated through, stirring constantly. Add milk if a thinner consistency is desired. Remove from the heat. Stir in the cheese. Sprinkle the reserved parsley over individual plates. Spoon the linguini over the parsley. Spoon the shrimp mixture over the linguini.

Yield: 4 servings

FETTUCCINI WITH
ASPARAGUS AND SHRIMP

1 pound asparagus
2 yellow bell peppers
1 large lemon
1 pound large shrimp, peeled, deveined
1/4 to 1/2 teaspoon crushed red pepper
1/2 teaspoon salt
12 ounces fettuccini or linguini
2 teaspoons salt
1 onion, chopped
1/2 teaspoon salt
2 tablespoons olive or vegetable oil
1/2 cup water
1 tablespoon soy sauce

Trim the asparagus and cut off any tough ends. Cut diagonally into 3-inch pieces. Cut the bell peppers into 1/4-inch-thick strips. Grate the lemon zest. Squeeze the juice from the lemon into a small bowl. Rinse the shrimp in cold water and pat dry.

Combine the shrimp, lemon juice, red pepper and 1/2 teaspoon salt in a bowl and mix well. Cook the fettuccini using the package directions and 2 teaspoons salt; drain. Return the fettuccini to the pot and keep warm.

Cook the onion, bell pepper and 1/2 teaspoon salt in 1 tablespoon of the olive oil in a nonstick 12-inch skillet over medium-high heat until bell peppers are tender-crisp.

Add the remaining 1 tablespoon olive oil to the skillet. Add the asparagus and shrimp mixture. Cook for 3 minutes or until asparagus are tender-crisp and shrimp turn pink. Stir in the bell pepper mixture and water. Cook until heated through.

Toss the fettuccini with the shrimp mixture and soy sauce in a large bowl. Sprinkle with lemon zest.

Yield: 6 servings

SHRIMP AND PASTA WITH CREAM SAUCE

1/4 cup (1/2 stick) butter or margarine
3 garlic cloves, minced
2 cups half-and-half
1 envelope parma rosa pasta sauce mix
2 tablespoons chopped fresh parsley
1/2 teaspoon salt
1/4 teaspoon pepper
3 ounces Parmesan cheese, grated
18 ounces small or medium frozen shrimp, thawed, drained
8 ounces angel hair pasta, cooked
3 ounces Parmesan cheese, grated

Heat the butter in a skillet until melted. Add the garlic and sauté until tender. Stir in the half-and-half. Cook over medium heat until heated through, stirring occasionally. Whisk in the sauce mix, parsley, salt and pepper. Simmer for 5 to 8 minutes, whisking occasionally.

Add 3 ounces cheese to the half-and-half mixture, stirring until cheese is melted. Stir in the shrimp. Cook over medium-low heat for 5 minutes or until shrimp turn pink. Place the pasta in a serving bowl. Spoon the shrimp mixture over the pasta. Sprinkle with 3 ounces cheese.

Yield: 4 to 6 servings

SHRIMP REMOULADE

1 cup mayonnaise
1 tablespoon chopped onion
1 tablespoon chopped celery
1 tablespoon chopped fresh parsley
2 tablespoons Dijon mustard
1 tablespoon horseradish
1 teaspoon paprika

1/2 teaspoon salt
Dash of Tabasco sauce
1/4 cup vegetable oil
1 tablespoon vinegar
1/2 teaspoon Worcestershire sauce
1 pound boiled shrimp

Combine the mayonnaise, onion, celery, parsley, Dijon mustard, horseradish, paprika, salt, Tabasco sauce, oil, vinegar and Worcestershire sauce in a bowl and mix well. Chill, covered, for 3 hours or longer. Place the shrimp in a serving bowl. Spoon the rémoulade sauce over the shrimp.

Yield: 4 servings

SHRIMP SCAMPI

1 cup (2 sticks) butter
1/2 cup lemon juice
1 garlic clove, minced
1 teaspoon parsley flakes
1 teaspoon Worcestershire
sauce
1 teaspoon soy sauce

1/2 teaspoon black pepper
1/4 teaspoon salt
1/4 teaspoon garlic salt
2 pounds large shrimp, peeled,
deveined
Lemon wedges for garnish

Heat the butter in a large skillet until melted. Add the lemon juice, garlic, parsley flakes, Worcestershire sauce, soy sauce, pepper, salt and garlic salt and mix well. Bring to a boil. Add the shrimp. Cook over medium heat for 5 minutes or until shrimp turn pink, stirring occasionally. Spoon onto a serving platter. Garnish with lemon wedges.

Yield: 6 to 8 servings

FRESH VEGETABLE PIZZA

1 (8-count) package crescent rolls
8 ounces cream cheese, softened
1¹/₂ teaspoons dillweed
1 cup mayonnaise
1¹/₂ teaspoons dried onion
¹/₄ cup finely chopped green olives
¹/₄ cup finely chopped black olives
¹/₄ cup finely chopped green bell pepper
¹/₂ cup finely chopped cauliflower
¹/₂ cup finely chopped broccoli
2 celery ribs, finely chopped
1 cup shredded mozzarella cheese

Unroll the crescent rolls on a greased baking sheet, stretching to the edges and pressing the perforations to seal. Bake at 400 degrees for 10 minutes or until golden. Let stand until cool.

Combine the cream cheese, dillweed, mayonnaise and onion in a bowl and mix well. Spread over the crust. Sprinkle the olives, bell pepper, cauliflower, broccoli and celery over the cream cheese mixture. Press into the cream cheese mixture. Sprinkle the cheese over the top. Chill, covered, for up to 1 week.

Yield: 4 servings

BLACK BEAN LASAGNA

1 (15-ounce) can black beans, rinsed
1/2 cup chopped onion
1/2 cup chopped green bell pepper
2 garlic cloves, minced
1 (15-ounce) can black beans, rinsed
1 (28-ounce) jar chunky tomato-onion-garlic sauce
1 1/2 cups low-fat cottage cheese
8 ounces reduced-fat cream cheese, softened
1/4 cup light sour cream
9 ready-to-use lasagna noodles

Mash 1 can black beans in a bowl. Sauté the onion, bell pepper and garlic in a skillet sprayed with nonstick cooking spray until tender. Stir in the mashed beans, 1 can black beans and sauce. Cook until heated through. Combine the cottage cheese, cream cheese and sour cream in a bowl and mix well.

Layer the noodles, bean mixture and cottage cheese mixture 1/3 at a time in a 3-quart rectangular baking dish sprayed with nonstick cooking spray. Bake, covered, at 350 degrees for 40 to 45 minutes.

Yield: 8 servings

HEALTHY VEGETABLE LASAGNA

8 ounces lasagna noodles
3 leeks, rinsed, chopped
3 carrots, peeled, sliced
3 garlic cloves, minced
8 ounces fresh mushrooms, sliced
1 (10-ounce) package frozen
chopped spinach, thawed,
drained
1 (10-ounce) package frozen
peas, thawed
1 (15-ounce) container low-fat
ricotta cheese
1/2 cup grated Parmesan cheese
1/4 cup egg substitute

4 ounces reduced-fat or light
mozzarella cheese, shredded
(about 1 cup)
1 tablespoon light margarine
1 tablespoon flour
1 (12-ounce) can evaporated
skim milk
1 (10-ounce) can fat-free cream
of mushroom or celery soup
Pinch of nutmeg
Salt and pepper to taste
2 tablespoons grated Parmesan
cheese

Cook the noodles using the package directions; drain. Sauté the leeks, carrots, garlic and mushrooms in a skillet sprayed with nonstick cooking spray over medium heat for 8 to 10 minutes or until tender. Drain the spinach, pressing out the excess moisture. Stir the spinach and peas into the vegetable mixture. Combine the ricotta cheese, 1/2 cup Parmesan cheese, egg substitute and mozzarella cheese in a bowl and mix well.

Heat the margarine in a small saucepan over medium heat until melted. Stir in the flour. Cook for 1 minute, stirring constantly. Whisk in the evaporated milk gradually. Bring to a boil. Cook for 1 to 2 minutes or until sauce is smooth and thickened, stirring constantly. Stir in the soup, nutmeg, salt and pepper and mix well.

Spoon enough of the milk mixture over the bottom of a 9×13-inch baking pan sprayed with nonstick cooking spray to cover. Layer 3 noodles, 1/2 the ricotta mixture and 1/2 of the vegetable mixture over the milk sauce. Drizzle with the milk sauce. Layer 3 noodles, remaining ricotta mixture and remaining vegetable mixture over the layers. Drizzle with the milk sauce. Arrange the remaining noodles over the layers. Pour the remaining milk sauce over the layers. Bake, covered, at 350 degrees for 45 to 50 minutes. Let stand for 10 minutes.

Sprinkle 2 tablespoons Parmesan cheese on a baking sheet. Toast in the oven for 5 minutes or until golden brown. Sprinkle over the top of the lasagna.

Yield: 12 servings

PASTA WITH ASPARAGUS AND LEMON CREAM

1 pound asparagus, trimmed
8 ounces fettuccini or penne pasta
1 cup heavy cream
1 tablespoon prepared horseradish
2 tablespoons chopped fresh dill, or 1 tablespoon dried dill
1 teaspoon grated lemon zest
1/2 cup grated Parmigiano-Reggiano cheese
Salt and pepper to taste

Cut the asparagus diagonally into 1/2-inch pieces. Cook the pasta using the package directions and adding the asparagus for the last 3 minutes; drain. Heat the cream, horseradish and dill in a large skillet over medium heat for 1 minute or until heated through. Add the cooked pasta and asparagus. Stir in the lemon zest and cheese. Season with salt and pepper. Cook until the cheese melts, stirring constantly.

Yield: 2 to 4 servings

SPINACH FETTUCCINI WITH MARINARA SAUCE

1 (12-ounce) package spinach fettuccini
2 (14-ounce) cans stewed tomatoes
1/2 cup chopped onion
1 teaspoon chopped garlic
1/2 teaspoon pepper
2 tablespoons olive oil
1/2 cup grated Parmesan cheese

Cook the fettuccini using the package directions. Drain and keep warm. Combine the tomatoes, onion, garlic, pepper and olive oil in a saucepan. Bring to a boil. Reduce the heat. Simmer for 10 minutes, stirring occasionally. Divide the fettuccini among the dinner plates. Spoon the sauce over the fettuccini. Sprinkle the cheese over the top. You may add shrimp to the sauce.

Yield: 4 to 6 servings

Side Dishes

ARKANSAS RIVER SAILING

Arkansas may be the smallest state west of the Mississippi River, but it holds a world of water-related recreation. The state offers clean, fresh water for fishing, swimming, canoeing, sailing, power boating, scuba diving, and more. There's always room for everyone along the 600,000 acres of lakes and almost 1,000 miles of streams.

SPICY BLACK BEANS WITH ONION AND BACON

4 ounces bacon, chopped
1 large onion, chopped
2 large garlic cloves, chopped
4 1/2 teaspoons chili powder
1 (4-ounce) can chopped
green chiles
2 (15-ounce) cans black beans,
drained, rinsed

2 teaspoons oregano
1/4 teaspoon cayenne pepper
1 (16-ounce) can chopped
peeled tomatoes
Salt to taste
Freshly ground black pepper
to taste

Cook the bacon in a large heavy saucepan over medium heat for 10 minutes or until light brown. Add the onion and garlic. Sauté for 5 minutes or until the onion is tender. Stir in the chili powder, green chiles, black beans, oregano, cayenne pepper and tomatoes. Bring to a simmer. Simmer for 12 minutes or until thick, stirring frequently. Season with salt and black pepper.

Yield: 4 servings

CORN CASSEROLE

1 (6-ounce) package corn
muffin mix
1 (16-ounce) can whole kernel
corn, drained
1 (17-ounce) can
cream-style corn
1 cup sour cream

2 eggs, beaten
1/2 cup (1 stick) butter,
melted
1/4 cup milk
1 tablespoon sugar
Dash of garlic powder
Salt and pepper to taste

Combine the corn muffin mix, corn, sour cream, eggs, butter, milk, sugar, garlic powder, salt and pepper in a bowl and mix well. Spoon into a greased 9×12-inch baking dish. Bake at 400 degrees for 45 minutes.

Yield: 8 to 12 servings

JALAPENO CORN

4 (16-ounce) cans whole kernel corn, drained
2 or 3 jalapeño chiles, chopped
1/4 cup (1/2 stick) margarine
8 ounces cream cheese
1 tablespoon sugar
Salt and pepper to taste

Combine the corn, jalapeño chiles, margarine, cream cheese, sugar, salt and pepper in a large saucepan. Bring to a boil, stirring constantly. Reduce the heat. Simmer for 30 minutes.

Yield: 8 to 10 servings

EGGPLANT CASSEROLE

1 eggplant
Salt to taste
2 tablespoons butter, softened
6 slices bread, toasted, crumbled
1/2 small onion, finely chopped
2 eggs
1 (10-ounce) can cream of mushroom soup
Salt and pepper to taste
1/2 cup shredded Cheddar cheese

Peel and cut the eggplant into slices. Place in a large bowl. Add enough cold water to cover. Sprinkle with salt. Let stand for 30 minutes. Drain and rinse the eggplant. Place the eggplant in a saucepan with enough water to cover. Sprinkle with salt. Cook, covered, until tender; drain.

Combine the cooked eggplant, butter, crumbled toast, onion, eggs, soup, salt, pepper and cheese in a bowl and mix well. Spoon into a buttered baking dish. Bake at 300 degrees for 30 to 40 minutes or until hot and bubbly.

Yield: 4 to 6 servings

ELEGANT EGGPLANT

1 (1- to 1^1/$_2$-pound) eggplant
2 tablespoons corn oil
^{1}/$_2$ cup chopped onion
^{1}/$_4$ cup chopped bell pepper
1 tomato, peeled, chopped
1 tablespoon finely chopped fresh basil, or ^{1}/$_4$ teaspoon dried basil
1 (4-ounce) can mushroom stems and pieces, drained
1 egg, beaten
1 cup shredded Cheddar cheese

Slice the eggplant in half lengthwise. Run a knife around the edge of each half, loosening the pulp from the skin. Cut through the pulp several times, being careful not to pierce the skin. Remove the pulp, reserving the skin. Cut the pulp into cubes. Bring enough water to cover the eggplant pulp to a boil in a saucepan. Add the eggplant. Cook for 10 minutes; drain.

Heat the corn oil in a 10-inch skillet. Add the onion and bell pepper. Cook until tender, stirring frequently. Stir in the tomato, basil, cooked eggplant and mushrooms. Stir a small amount of the eggplant mixture into the egg. Stir the egg into the hot eggplant mixture. Cook until mixture thickens, stirring frequently. Remove from the heat. Spoon into the reserved eggplant shells. Sprinkle the cheese over the top. Place on a baking sheet. Bake at 375 degrees for 25 minutes. You may substitute 8 ounces fresh sliced mushrooms that have been sautéed and drained for the can of mushroom stems and pieces.

Yield: 4 servings

OKRA AND CORN SURPRISE

1/2 cup chopped onion
1/2 cup chopped bell pepper
2 tablespoons bacon drippings
1 (10-ounce) can tomatoes
with green chiles
1 teaspoon flour

2 (16-ounce) cans whole
kernel corn, drained
1 (8-ounce) can tomato paste
1 cup chopped okra
Salt and pepper to taste

Sauté the onion and bell pepper in the bacon drippings in a large skillet until brown. Combine the tomatoes with green chiles and flour in a bowl and mix well. Add to the onion mixture. Add the corn and tomato paste to the onion mixture and mix well. Simmer for 15 minutes. Add the okra. Simmer for 15 minutes or until okra is tender. Season with salt and pepper.

Yield: 6 to 8 servings

GREEN BEANS IN SOUR CREAM

2 (20-ounce) cans whole green
beans, drained
1 onion, separated into rings
1 tablespoon vinegar
1 tablespoon vegetable oil
Salt and pepper to taste
1 cup sour cream

1/2 cup mayonnaise
1 tablespoon lemon juice
1/4 teaspoon (heaping) dry
mustard
1 teaspoon horseradish
1 teaspoon onion juice
2 teaspoons chopped chives

Combine the beans, onion rings, vinegar and oil in a bowl and toss to combine. Sprinkle with salt and pepper. Marinate, covered, for 1 to 12 hours. Combine the sour cream, mayonnaise, lemon juice, dry mustard, horseradish, onion juice and chives and mix well. Add to the green bean mixture and mix well.

Yield: 6 to 8 servings

BACON WRAPPED GREEN BEANS

BACON WRAPPED GREEN BEANS

1 pound bacon slices
2 (16-ounce) cans whole green
beans, drained
6 tablespoons margarine,
melted

1/2 cup packed brown sugar
Garlic salt to taste
Salt and pepper to taste

Cut the bacon slices into halves. Wrap 6 or 7 green beans with a piece of bacon, securing with a wooden pick. Place in a 9×13-inch baking dish. Repeat with the remaining bacon pieces and green beans until all ingredients are used. Combine the margarine, brown sugar, garlic salt, salt and pepper in a bowl and mix well. Pour over the bacon-wrapped green beans. Bake, covered, at 375 degrees for 40 minutes. Remove the cover. Bake for 5 minutes longer.

Yield: 4 to 6 servings

ONION CASSEROLE

3 sweet onions
2 tablespoons margarine
8 ounces fresh mushrooms, sliced
1 cup shredded Swiss cheese
1 (10-ounce) can cream of
mushroom soup

1 (5-ounce) can evaporated milk
2 teaspoons soy sauce
6 (1/2-inch-thick) slices
French bread
1 cup shredded Swiss cheese
1/4 cup chopped fresh parsley

Cut the onions into slices. Cut the onion slices crosswise. Heat the margarine in a skillet until melted. Add the onions and mushrooms. Cook until tender, stirring frequently. Spoon into a 9×12-inch baking dish. Sprinkle 1 cup cheese over the onion mixture. Combine the soup, milk and soy sauce in a bowl and mix well. Pour over the layers. Arrange the bread slices over the layers. Sprinkle with 1 cup cheese and parsley. Chill, covered, for 4 to 8 hours. Let stand at room temperature for 30 minutes. Bake, covered, at 375 degrees for 30 minutes. Remove the cover. Bake for 15 to 20 minutes longer.

Yield: 6 servings

POTATO AND PARMESAN GRATIN

2 1/2 pounds russet potatoes, peeled, cut into 1/8-inch-thick slices
Salt and pepper to taste
1/4 cup (1/2 stick) butter, melted
2 cups packed freshly grated Parmesan cheese
2 cups whole milk

Layer the potatoes, salt, pepper, butter and cheese one-third at a time in a buttered 9X13-inch baking dish. Pour the milk evenly over the layers. Bake in a preheated 400-degree oven for 15 minutes. Reduce the temperature to 350 degrees. Bake for 1 hour or until potatoes are tender, top is golden brown and most of the milk is absorbed. Let stand for 10 minutes.

Yield: 6 servings

TWICE-BAKED POTATO CASSEROLE

6 to 8 potatoes
1 cup sour cream
1/2 cup (1 stick) butter, softened
12 ounces Cheez Whiz
2 hard-cooked eggs, chopped
3 green onions, chopped
8 ounces crisp-cooked bacon, crumbled
Salt and pepper to taste

Combine the potatoes with enough water to cover in a saucepan. Bring to a boil. Boil until tender; drain. Mash the potatoes in a large bowl. Add the sour cream, butter, Cheez Whiz, eggs, green onions, bacon, salt and pepper and mix well. Spoon into a baking dish. Bake at 350 degrees for 30 minutes or until bubbly.

Yield: 6 to 8 servings

SQUASH CASSEROLE

8 yellow squash, thinly sliced
1/2 cup chopped onion
1/2 cup (1 stick) butter, melted
1 (16-ounce) package shredded Velveeta Mexican cheese
1 (12-ounce) package butter crackers, crushed
1/4 cup (1/2 stick) butter, melted
Pepper to taste

Combine the squash slices, onion and 1/2 cup melted butter in a bowl and mix gently. Spoon evenly into a greased baking dish. Sprinkle the cheese over the squash mixture. Sprinkle the butter crackers over the cheese. Drizzle 1/4 cup melted butter over the butter crackers. Sprinkle with pepper. Bake at 350 degrees for 15 to 20 minutes or until cracker crumbs are golden brown.

Yield: 10 to 12 servings

MARINATED BUTTERNUT SQUASH

2 butternut squash, cut into halves, seeded
Kosher salt to taste
Freshly ground black pepper to taste
1/2 cup extra-virgin olive oil
1/4 cup red wine vinegar
1/2 red onion, thinly sliced
1/2 teaspoon hot red pepper flakes
1 tablespoon oregano
1 garlic clove, thinly sliced
1/4 cup chopped fresh mint leaves

Cut the squash crosswise into 1-inch-thick slices. Arrange in a single layer on 1 or 2 baking sheets. Sprinkle with Kosher salt and black pepper. Drizzle with 1/4 cup of the olive oil. Roast at 450 degrees for 18 to 20 minutes or just until tender. Let stand until cool. Place in a shallow dish. Mix the remaining 1/4 cup olive oil, and the next 5 ingredients in a bowl. Season with Kosher salt and black pepper. Pour over the squash. Let stand for 20 minutes to 6 hours; do not chill. Sprinkle with the mint.

Yield: 8 to 12 servings

CREAM SPINACH

2 cups heavy cream
6 tablespoons chopped
   smoked bacon
1/4 cup finely chopped onion
   Butter
3 tablespoons vegetable oil

2 handfuls baby spinach,
   trimmed
1/4 cup coarsely chopped,
   seeded, skinned tomatoes
Salt and freshly ground
   black pepper to taste

Cook the cream in a saucepan until reduced to 1/2 cup. Cook the bacon in a skillet until lightly browned. Cook the onion in a small amount of butter in a skillet until tender. Heat the oil in a separate skillet over medium heat. Add the spinach. Stir in the cream, bacon, onion and tomatoes. Season with salt and pepper. Serve immediately.

Yield: 4 servings

SPINACH MADELINE

2 (10-ounce) packages frozen
   chopped spinach
1/4 cup (1/2 stick) butter
2 tablespoons flour
2 tablespoons chopped onion
1/2 cup evaporated milk
1/2 teaspoon black pepper
3/4 teaspoon celery salt

3/4 teaspoon garlic salt
1 (6-ounce) jalapeño cheese
   roll, cut into small pieces
1 teaspoon Worcestershire
   sauce
Red pepper to taste
Buttered bread crumbs
   (optional)

Cook the spinach using the package directions. Drain and reserve the liquid. Add enough water to the reserved liquid to measure 1/2 cup. Heat the butter in a saucepan over low heat until melted. Add the flour, stirring until smooth; do not brown. Add the onion and cook until tender. Stir in the reserved liquid and milk gradually. Cook until thickened, stirring constantly. Add the black pepper, celery salt, garlic salt, cheese, Worcestershire sauce and red pepper. Cook until cheese is melted, stirring frequently. Stir in the cooked spinach. Spoon into a serving bowl. For enhanced flavor spoon into a baking dish and top with buttered bread crumbs. Chill, covered, for 8 to 12 hours. Bake at 350 degrees until hot and bubbly. You may freeze this dish.

Yield: 4 to 6 servings

SWEET POTATOES WITH PINEAPPLE

1 (16-ounce) can sweet potatoes, drained
1/2 cup (1 stick) butter, melted
1/2 cup packed brown sugar
1/4 cup sugar
1/2 teaspoon pumpkin pie spice
1 (8-ounce) can crushed pineapple, drained
3/4 cup nuts (optional)
Dash of salt
Marshmallows (optional)

Mash the sweet potatoes in a large bowl. Add the butter, brown sugar, sugar, pumpkin pie spice, pineapple, nuts and salt and mix well. Spoon into a baking dish. Bake at 375 degrees for 25 minutes. Arrange the marshmallows over the top. Bake for 5 minutes or until marshmallows are light brown.

Yield: 4 to 6 servings

MARINATED TOMATOES

4 cups sliced peeled tomatoes
1 garlic clove, minced
1 teaspoon salt
1 teaspoon sugar
1/8 teaspoon cayenne pepper
2 tablespoons tarragon vinegar
2 teaspoons mustard
1/4 cup vegetable oil
1/4 cup parsley flakes

Arrange the tomato slices evenly in a 9×12-inch glass dish. Combine the garlic, salt, sugar, cayenne pepper, vinegar, mustard, oil and parsley flakes in a bowl and mix well. Pour over the tomato slices. Chill, covered, for 4 to 5 hours.

Yield: 6 to 8 servings

TOMATO PIE

1 cup mayonnaise
1 cup freshly grated Parmesan
cheese
2 tablespoons flour

3 or 4 thinly sliced tomatoes
1 unbaked pie shell
Chopped fresh or dried parsley to taste

Combine the mayonnaise, cheese and flour in a bowl and mix well. Layer the mayonnaise mixture and tomatoes $1/2$ at a time in the pie shell. Sprinkle with the parsley. Bake at 400 degrees for 30 to 40 minutes or until set. Serve warm.

Yield: 6 servings

VEGETABLE CASSEROLE

2 green bell peppers, sliced
1 potato, chopped
2 small carrots, thinly sliced
1 onion, chopped
1 zucchini, chopped
3 tablespoons chopped
fresh parsley
4 large tomatoes, sliced

1 cup rice
1 tablespoon salt
1 teaspoon pepper
$1/2$ cup water
$1/2$ cup vegetable oil
1 teaspoon Tabasco sauce
2 teaspoons vinegar
1 cup shredded cheese

Combine the bell peppers, potato, carrots, onion, zucchini and parsley in a bowl and mix well. Layer $1/2$ the tomato slices, $1/2$ the vegetable mixture, the rice, the remaining vegetable mixture and the remaining tomato slices in an oiled 9×13-inch baking pan. Combine the salt, pepper, water, oil, Tabasco sauce and vinegar in a bowl and mix well. Pour over the layers. Bake, covered, at 350 degrees for a metal pan or at 325 degrees for a glass dish for 2 hours. Remove the cover. Sprinkle the cheese over the top. Bake until the cheese melts. You may brown the casserole under the broiler.

Yield: 10 to 12 servings

VEGETABLE CASSEROLE WITH CHEESE SAUCE

1 head cauliflower
1 bunch broccoli
8 ounces carrots, coarsely chopped
Salt and pepper to taste
1 1/2 (10-ounce) cans cream of mushroom soup
1/2 cup (1 stick) butter or margarine, softened
1/2 teaspoon garlic salt
8 ounces Velveeta cheese, cubed
1 (6-ounce) can French-fried onions

Cut the florets from the cauliflower and broccoli. Steam the florets and carrots until tender-crisp; drain. Arrange evenly in a baking dish. Sprinkle with salt and pepper. Combine the soup, butter, and garlic salt in a bowl and mix well. Stir in the cheese. Spoon over the vegetables. Sprinkle the onions over the top. Bake at 350 degrees for 20 minutes. You may substitute a frozen vegetable medley for the cauliflower, broccoli and carrots.

Yield: 10 to 12 servings

FRIED ZUCCHINI

5 zucchini
Cornmeal
2 tablespoons vegetable oil
1/2 onion, chopped
Seasoned salt
1 (10-ounce) can tomatoes with green chiles
1/2 to 3/4 cup shredded Cheddar cheese
Salt and pepper to taste

Peel the zucchini and cut into julienne slices. Place the cornmeal in a shallow dish. Dredge the zucchini in the cornmeal to coat. Heat the oil in a skillet. Add the zucchini and onion. Sprinkle with the seasoned salt. Sauté over medium-high heat until lightly browned and zucchini is tender-crisp. Stir in the tomatoes and cheese. Reduce the heat. Season with salt and pepper. Cook until cheese is melted, stirring frequently.

Yield: 10 to 12 servings

CURRIED FRUIT

1 (29-ounce) can peach halves, drained
1 (17-ounce) can apricots, drained
1 (29-ounce) can pears, drained
3 (8-ounce) cans pineapple tidbits, drained
10 maraschino cherries
1/3 cup butter, melted
3/4 cup packed brown sugar
2 to 4 teaspoons curry powder

Arrange the peach halves, apricots, pears, pineapple tidbits and cherries, cut side up, in a baking dish. Combine the butter, brown sugar and enough curry powder to make of the desired taste in a bowl and mix well. Spread over the fruit. Bake at 325 degrees for 1 hour. Chill, covered, for 1 day. Bake at 300 degrees for 30 minutes or until heated through.

Yield: 12 to 15 servings

FIESTA RICE

4 teaspoons butter
1 cup chopped red bell pepper
1 cup chopped yellow bell pepper
1 cup chopped green bell pepper
1 cup finely chopped sweet onion
4 garlic cloves, minced
2 cups rice
1/2 teaspoon ground Mexican oregano
1 teaspoon cumin
2 teaspoons cilantro
6 cups chicken stock
2 teaspoons minced fresh parsley for garnish

Heat the butter in a large skillet until melted. Add the bell peppers, onion, garlic, rice, oregano, cumin and cilantro. Sauté until rice is coated and golden brown, stirring frequently. Stir in the stock. Bring to a boil. Reduce the heat. Simmer, covered, for 15 minutes. Remove from the heat. Stir and set the lid ajar. Let stand for 5 minutes. Garnish with the parsley.

Yield: 8 to 12 servings

POPPY SEED RICE

1/4 cup (1/2 stick) butter
1 1/2 cups rice
1 onion, finely chopped
1/8 teaspoon pepper
3 cups beef consommé
2 tablespoons poppy seeds
1/2 cup slivered almonds
3 (3-ounce) cans mushrooms, drained (optional)

Heat the butter in a heavy skillet until melted. Add the rice and cook until browned. Add the onion and pepper. Cook until onion is tender, stirring frequently. Remove from the heat. Stir in the consommé, poppy seeds, almonds and mushrooms. Spoon into a buttered 2-quart baking dish. Bake at 375 degrees for 1 hour.

Yield: 8 to 10 servings

GARLIC CHEESE GRITS

1 cup quick-cooking grits
1 (6-ounce) roll garlic cheese
1/2 cup (1 stick) butter
2 eggs, beaten
3/4 cup milk

Cook the grits using the package directions. Add the garlic cheese and butter, stirring until melted. Combine the eggs and milk in a bowl. Stir into the grits mixture. Spoon into a buttered baking dish. Bake at 375 degrees for 1 hour.

Yield: 4 to 6 servings

Cookies and Pies

ARKANSAS RIVER AT SUNSET

The Arkansas River is a haven for people who like to fish. Largemouth and smallmouth bass, bream, crappie, and catfish flourish in this major mid-American fishery. Don't want to fish? Travel to the Little Rock and North Little Rock riverwalks to check out restaurants, a farmers' market, a variety of specialty shops, and outdoor concerts. See college basketball, professional hockey, arena football, or the latest star in concert at the ALLTEL Arena by the Arkansas River in North Little Rock. The Natural State offers it all.

EASTER STORY COOKIES

(To Be Made the Night Before Easter)

1 cup whole pecans	Pinch of salt
1 teaspoon vinegar	1 cup sugar
3 egg whites	

Preheat the oven to 300 degrees. Place the pecans in a sealable plastic bag. Let children beat them with a wooden spoon to break into small pieces. Explain that after Jesus was arrested, He was beaten by Roman soldiers. John 19:1-3.

Let each child smell the vinegar. Place 1 teaspoon vinegar into a bowl. Explain that when Jesus was thirsty on the cross, He was given vinegar to drink. John 19:28-30.

Add the egg whites to the vinegar. Eggs represent life. Explain that Jesus gave His life to give us life. John 10:10-11.

Sprinkle salt into each child's hand. Let them taste it and brush the rest into the bowl. Explain that this represents the salty tears shed by Jesus' followers and the bitterness of our own sin. Luke 23:27.

Add the sugar. Explain that the sweetest part of the story is that Jesus died because He loves us. He wants to know us and for us to belong to Him. Psalms 34:8 and John 3:16.

Beat with a mixer on high for 12 to 15 minutes or until stiff peaks form. Explain that the color white represents the purity in God's eyes of those whose sins have been cleansed by Jesus. Isaiah 1:18 and John 3:1-3.

Fold in the broken nuts. Drop by teaspoonfuls onto a waxed paper-lined cookie sheet. Explain that each mound represents the rocky tomb where Jesus was laid to rest. Matthew 27:57-60.

Put the cookie sheet in the oven and close the door. Turn the oven off and seal the door. Explain that Jesus' tomb was sealed. Matthew 27:65-66.

Go to Bed! Explain that they may feel sad to leave the cookies in the oven overnight. Jesus' followers were in despair when the tomb was sealed. John 16:20-22.

Easter Morning! Open the oven and give everyone a cookie. Notice the cracked surface and take a bite. The cookies are hollow! On the first Easter, Jesus' followers were amazed to find the tomb open and empty! Matthew 28:1-9.

COWBOY COOKIES

2 cups flour

1 1/2 teaspoons baking soda

1/4 teaspoon salt

1 teaspoon baking powder

1 cup (2 sticks) margarine, softened

1 cup sugar

1 cup packed brown sugar

2 eggs, beaten

2 to 3 tablespoons honey

2 teaspoons vanilla extract

2 cups oats

1 1/2 cups semisweet chocolate or butterscotch chips

1 cup chopped nuts

Sift the flour, baking soda, salt and baking powder together. Cream the margarine, sugar and brown sugar in a mixing bowl until light and fluffy. Add the eggs, honey and vanilla and mix well. Add the sifted dry ingredients and mix well. Stir in the oats, chocolate chips and nuts. Drop by teaspoonfuls 2 inches apart onto a greased cookie sheet. Bake at 325 degrees for 15 minutes. Cool on a wire rack.

Yield: 3 to 4 dozen cookies

NO-BAKE COOKIES

1/2 cup (1 stick) butter or margarine, softened

1/2 cup milk

2 cups sugar

1/2 cup baking cocoa

1/2 cup quick-cooking oats

1/2 cup peanut butter

1 teaspoon vanilla extract

Combine the butter, milk, sugar and baking cocoa in a saucepan. Bring to a boil, stirring constantly. Boil for 1 minute. Remove from the heat. Stir in the oats, peanut butter and vanilla. Drop by teaspoonfuls onto waxed paper. Let stand until cooled completely. Remove from the waxed paper and place in an airtight container.

Yield: 1 to 2 dozen cookies

OATMEAL COOKIES

1¹/4 cups flour
1 teaspoon baking soda
1 cup (2 sticks) butter or margarine, softened
¹/4 cup sugar
³/4 cup packed light brown sugar
1 (4-ounce) package vanilla instant pudding mix
2 eggs
3¹/2 cups quick-cooking rolled oats
1 cup raisins (optional)

Combine the flour and baking soda in a bowl and mix well. Cream the butter, sugar, brown sugar and pudding mix in a mixing bowl until light and fluffy. Beat in the eggs. Add the flour mixture gradually, mixing well after each addition. Stir in the oats and raisins; batter will be stiff. Drop by teaspoonfuls 2 inches apart onto a cookie sheet. Bake at 375 degrees for 10 to 12 minutes or until light brown. Cool on a wire rack.

Yield: 3 dozen cookies

PEANUT BUTTER OATMEAL COOKIES

¹/2 cup (1 stick) butter, softened
1¹/2 cups packed brown sugar
1 cup sugar
4 eggs
1 teaspoon vanilla extract
2 cups peanut butter
6 cups rolled oats
2¹/2 teaspoons baking soda

Cream the butter, brown sugar and sugar in a mixing bowl until light and fluffy. Add the eggs and vanilla and mix well. Add the peanut butter and mix well. Stir in the oats and baking soda. Drop by tablespoonfuls onto a cookie sheet. Flatten slightly with a fork. Bake at 350 degrees for 12 to 14 minutes or until light brown. Cool on the cookie sheet. You may drop by ¹/4 cupfuls onto a cookie sheet and bake for 14 minutes or until light brown.

Yield: 5 to 6 dozen cookies

POLKA DOT COOKIES

1 (22-ounce) package brownie mix
1/2 cup vegetable oil
2 eggs
1 cup white chocolate chips or vanilla-milk chocolate chips

Combine the brownie mix, oil and eggs in a bowl and mix well. Stir in the chocolate chips. Drop by spoonfuls onto a cookie sheet. Bake at 350 degrees for 10 minutes. Cool on a wire rack.

Yield: 2 to 3 dozen cookies

SNICKERDOODLES

2 3/4 cups sifted flour
2 teaspoons cream of tartar
1 teaspoon baking soda
1/2 teaspoon salt
1 cup (2 sticks) butter or shortening
1 1/2 cups sugar
2 eggs
5 tablespoons sugar
2 teaspoons cinnamon

Sift the flour, cream of tartar, baking soda and salt together. Cream the butter and 1 1/2 cups sugar in a mixing bowl until light and fluffy. Beat in the eggs. Add the flour mixture and mix well. Chill in the refrigerator.

Combine 5 tablespoons sugar and cinnamon in a bowl and mix well. Shape the chilled dough into small balls. Roll in the sugar mixture to coat. Place 2 inches apart on a cookie sheet. Bake at 400 degrees for 6 to 8 minutes or until lightly browned and soft.

Yield: 2 to 3 dozen cookies

VANILLA BUTTERSCOTCH CHIP COOKIES

2 cups flour
1 teaspoon baking powder
1/4 teaspoon salt
1 cup sugar
1/3 cup vegetable oil
2 eggs
1 teaspoon vanilla extract
1 (10-ounce) package butterscotch or vanilla chips
Sugar

Combine the flour, baking powder and salt in a bowl and mix well. Combine the sugar, oil, eggs and vanilla in a separate bowl and mix well. Add the flour mixture gradually, mixing well after each addition. Stir in the butterscotch chips. Shape into 1-inch balls. Roll in sugar to coat. Place on a cookie sheet. Bake at 350 degrees for 8 to 10 minutes or until tops crack; do not brown.

Yield: 4 dozen cookies

CARAMEL BROWNIES

1 cup (2 sticks) butter
1 (16-ounce) package brown sugar
1 cup sugar
4 eggs
1 teaspoon vanilla extract
1 teaspoon baking powder
2 cups flour
Chopped nuts (optional)
Confectioners' sugar

Combine the butter, brown sugar and sugar in a saucepan. Cook until butter melts, stirring constantly. Let stand until cool. Add the eggs, vanilla, baking powder and flour and mix well. Stir in the nuts. Pour into a 9×13-inch baking pan. Bake at 350 degrees for 20 to 30 minutes or until brownies pull from the sides of the pan. Let stand until cool. Cut into squares. Sprinkle with confectioners' sugar.

Yield: 2 dozen brownies

MARBLED DOUBLE CHOCOLATE CHEESECAKE SQUARES

1 cup flour
1/4 cup baking cocoa
1/2 cup (1 stick) butter, softened
1/2 cup sugar
1/4 teaspoon salt
16 ounces cream cheese, softened
1/2 cup sugar
2 eggs
2 teaspoons vanilla extract
1/2 cup chocolate topping, room temperature
1/4 cup semisweet chocolate chips, melted

Line an 8- or 9-inch square baking pan with foil extending the edges over the sides of the pan. Combine the flour and baking cocoa in a bowl and mix well. Beat the butter, 1/2 cup sugar and salt in a separate bowl until smooth. Beat in the flour mixture gradually, beating until a soft dough is formed. Press over the bottom of the prepared pan.

Beat the cream cheese and 1/2 cup sugar in a mixing bowl until smooth. Add the eggs and vanilla and mix well.

Combine 1 cup of the cream cheese mixture with the chocolate topping in a bowl and mix well. Spoon 1 cup of the chocolate topping mixture over the dough layer. Combine the remaining chocolate topping mixture with the melted chocolate chips and mix well. Set aside.

Pour the remaining cream cheese mixture 1/4 cup at a time over the layers. Spoon the chocolate mixture over the top. Cut with a knife, through the batter layers, creating a marbled effect.

Bake at 350 degrees for 35 to 40 minutes or until firm and slightly puffed. Cool completely in the pan on a wire rack. Refrigerate, covered, until completely chilled. Lift from the pan using the foil edges.

Yield: 20 squares

CRUNCHY PEANUT BARS

1 (2-layer) package yellow cake mix
1/3 cup butter, melted
1 egg, beaten
3 cups miniature marshmallows
2 cups peanut butter chips
2/3 cup corn syrup
1/4 cup (1/2 stick) butter
2 teaspoons vanilla extract
2 cups crisp rice cereal
2 cups salted peanuts

Combine the cake mix, melted butter and egg in a bowl and mix well. Spread evenly over the bottom of a 9×13-inch baking pan. Bake at 350 degrees for 12 to 18 minutes or until golden brown. Arrange the marshmallows over the hot layer. Combine the peanut butter chips, corn syrup, butter and vanilla in a saucepan. Cook until peanut butter chips and butter are melted, stirring constantly. Stir in the cereal and peanuts. Spoon over the marshmallows. Let stand until firm.

Yield: 2 to 3 dozen bars

GERMAN CHOCOLATE BARS

1 (2-layer) package German chocolate cake mix
1 cup flaked coconut
1 cup pecans, chopped
1/2 cup (1 stick) margarine or butter, softened
2 eggs
1 (16-ounce) package confectioners' sugar
8 ounces cream cheese, softened
1/2 cup (1 stick) margarine or butter, softened

Combine the cake mix, coconut, pecans, 1/2 cup margarine and eggs in a bowl and mix well. Spoon evenly over the bottom of a large glass baking dish. Cream the confectioners' sugar, cream cheese and 1/2 cup margarine in a bowl until light and fluffy. Spread over the batter. Bake at 350 degrees for 1 hour.

Yield: 2 to 3 dozen bars

KUNCHEN BARS

1 (2-layer) package yellow cake mix
1/2 cup (1 stick) butter, melted
1/2 cup flaked coconut
1 (21-ounce) can apple or cherry pie filling
1/2 cup sour cream
1 egg

Combine the cake mix, butter and coconut in a bowl and mix well. Spread over the bottom of a greased 9×13-inch cake pan. Bake at 350 degrees for 10 minutes. Spread the pie filling over the baked layer. Beat the sour cream and egg together in a bowl. Drizzle over the pie filling layer. Bake at 350 degrees for 30 minutes.

Yield: 2 to 3 dozen bars

LEMON SQUARES

2 cups flour
1/2 cup confectioners' sugar
1 cup (2 sticks) butter
4 eggs
1/4 cup lemon juice
2 cups sugar
1/4 cup flour

Combine 2 cups flour and confectioners' sugar in a bowl and mix well. Cut in the butter until crumbly. Press over the bottom of a 9×13-inch baking pan. Bake at 325 degrees for 25 to 30 minutes or until light brown. Cool on a wire rack.

Beat the eggs in a mixing bowl until foamy. Beat in the lemon juice. Combine the sugar and 1/4 cup flour in a bowl and mix well. Add to the egg mixture and mix well. Pour over the cooled crust. Bake at 325 degrees for 25 to 30 minutes or until set. Sprinkle confectioners' sugar over the top while warm. Cool on a wire rack.

Yield: 2 to 3 dozen squares

CRISPY CRUNCH

2 cups chocolate chips
1 cup peanut butter
1/2 cup (1 stick) butter or margarine
1 (12-ounce) package Crispix cereal
1 (16-ounce) package confectioners' sugar

Heat the chocolate chips, peanut butter and butter in a saucepan until melted, stirring constantly. Stir in the Crispix. Dredge the pieces in confectioners' sugar to coat.

Yield: 2 dozen pieces

MILLIONAIRE CANDY

1 (14-ounce) package caramels
1/4 cup evaporated milk
2 cups pecan halves
1 (20-ounce) chocolate candy bar
1/3 block paraffin

Place the caramels and evaporated milk in a double boiler over simmering water. Cook until caramels are melted. Stir in the pecans. Drop by spoonfuls onto a greased baking sheet. Chill in the refrigerator.

Place the candy bar and paraffin in a double boiler over simmering water. Cook until candy bar and paraffin are melted. Dip each piece of candy in the chocolate and place on waxed paper until firm.

Yield: 2 dozen candies

ORANGE SNOW BALLS

2³/4 cups vanilla wafer crumbs
1/4 cup (1/2 stick) butter, melted
1 cup confectioners' sugar
1 cup chopped nuts
1/4 cup frozen orange juice concentrate, thawed
Butter Icing

Combine the wafer crumbs, butter, confectioners' sugar, nuts and orange juice concentrate in a bowl and mix well. Shape into small balls. Dip each ball in Butter Icing. Place on a baking sheet. Store in the refrigerator.

Yield: 2 to 3 dozen candies

BUTTER ICING

2 tablespoons margarine, softened
2 cups confectioners' sugar
Milk
Flaked coconut to taste

Combine the margarine, confectioners' sugar and enough milk to make of a thin consistency in a bowl and mix well. Stir in the coconut.

PEPPERMINT FUDGE

2¹/2 cups sugar
1/2 cup (1 stick) butter
2/3 cup evaporated milk
1 (7-ounce) jar marshmallow creme
8 ounces white almond bark
1/2 cup finely crushed peppermint stick candy
Red food coloring

Line a 9×13-inch dish with foil. Combine the sugar, butter and evaporated milk in a saucepan. Bring to a boil, stirring constantly. Boil for 5 minutes. Remove from the heat. Add the marshmallow creme and almond bark and stir until smooth. Add the candy and enough food coloring to make of the desired shade of pink. Pour into the prepared pan. Let stand until cool. Cut into squares.

Yield: 3 dozen pieces

NUT SMACKERS

1 egg white
3/4 cup packed light brown sugar
2 tablespoons sifted self-rising flour
1/2 teaspoon vanilla extract
2 cups pecan halves

Line a baking sheet with foil. Coat the baking sheet with vegetable oil. Beat the egg white in a bowl until soft peaks form. Fold in the brown sugar, flour and vanilla. Dip each pecan half into the mixture with a fork, turning to cover. Place 1 inch apart on the prepared baking sheet. Bake at 250 degrees for 30 minutes. Cool on a wire rack.

Yield: 8 servings

EASY CARAMEL PIE

10 caramel candies
1/3 cup flour
3 cups (1/2-inch cubes) Jonathan or Rome apples
2/3 cup caramel ice cream topping
2 teaspoons lemon juice
1 frozen unbaked (9-inch) pie shell
1/2 cup pecan pieces

Heat a baking sheet in a 375-degree oven. Cut each caramel into 4 pieces. Combine with the flour in a bowl and toss to coat the caramels. Add the apples, topping and lemon juice and mix well. Spoon into the pie shell. Sprinkle with the pecans. Place on the hot baking sheet. Bake for 40 to 45 minutes. Store at room temperature.

Yield: 6 to 8 servings

CHERRY NUT PIE

1 (14-ounce) can sweetened condensed milk
1 (15-ounce) can sour red pitted cherries, drained, chopped
1 cup pecans, chopped
1 cup whipping cream, whipped, or 8 ounces nondairy whipped topping
Juice of 2 small lemons (about 2 tablespoons)
1 graham cracker pie shell

Combine the condensed milk, cherries and pecans in a bowl and mix well. Stir in the whipped cream and lemon juice. Chill in the refrigerator. Spoon into the pie shell.

Yield: 6 to 8 servings

LEMONADE PIE

1 (14-ounce) can sweetened condensed milk
1 (6-ounce) can frozen lemonade concentrate, thawed
12 ounces nondairy whipped topping
2 (9-inch) graham cracker pie shells

Combine the condensed milk and lemonade concentrate in a bowl and mix well. Set aside 1/2 cup of the whipped topping. Fold the remaining whipped topping into the lemonade mixture. Pour the filling into the pie shells. Place a 1/4-cup dollop of the reserved whipped topping on the center of each pie. Freeze, covered, in the freezer. Serve frozen. You may garnish the pies with lemon twists or mint leaves.

Yield: 12 to 16 servings

OREO PIE

1 (1-pound) package chocolate sandwich cookies, crushed
1/2 cup (1 stick) butter, melted
8 ounces cream cheese, softened
1 cup confectioners' sugar
16 ounces nondairy whipped topping
1 (6-ounce) package chocolate instant pudding mix

Sprinkle half of the cookie crumbs over the bottom of a 9×13-inch dish. Pour the butter over the crumbs and press down to combine. Combine the cream cheese, confectioners' sugar and half of the whipped topping in a bowl and mix well. Spread over the cookie layer.

Prepare the pudding using the package directions. Spread over the cream cheese layer. Spread the remaining whipped topping over the pudding layer. Sprinkle the remaining cookie crumbs over the top. Chill, covered, until firm.

Yield: 2 to 3 dozen servings

SWEDISH APPLE PIE

2 cups sliced apples
2 tablespoons flour
1/3 cup sugar
Pinch of salt
1 egg
1 teaspoon vanilla extract
1 cup sour cream
1 unbaked (9-inch) pie shell
1/3 cup sugar
1/3 cup flour
1 teaspoon cinnamon
1/2 cup (1 stick) butter

Combine the apples, 2 tablespoons flour, 1/3 cup sugar, salt, egg, vanilla and sour cream in a bowl and mix well. Spoon into the pie shell. Bake at 350 degrees for 30 minutes.

Combine 1/3 cup sugar, 1/3 cup flour and cinnamon in a bowl and mix well. Cut in the butter until crumbly. Sprinkle evenly over the pie. Bake for 15 minutes longer.

Yield: 6 to 8 servings

Cakes and Desserts

The dedication of the McClellan-Kerr Arkansas River Navigation System in 1971 culminated the largest civil works project ever carried out by the U.S. Army Corps of Engineers up to that time. The flood-prone Arkansas River now flows peaceably by farm fields of south Arkansas, central Arkansas' Pinnacle Mountain State Park, and the historic frontier town of Fort Smith en route to Oklahoma. Today, hundreds of tows traverse the River each year en route to the Mississippi River, to New Orleans, and around the world. Fishermen find world-class fishing, while tourists find exciting festivals and other activities along the riverfront.

APPLE IRISH CREAM CAKE

3¹/₂ cups flour

1 tablespoon baking soda

2 teaspoons cinnamon

1 teaspoon salt

1 teaspoon nutmeg

¹/₂ teaspoon ground cardamom

1¹/₄ cups (2¹/₂ sticks)
unsalted butter, softened

1¹/₂ cups packed dark
brown sugar

1 cup sugar

3 eggs

3/4 cup Irish cream liqueur

1/4 cup dark rum

3 cups finely chopped apples

1¹/₂ cups chopped pecans,
toasted (about 6 ounces)

6 tablespoons Irish cream
liqueur

Irish Cream Glaze

Sift the flour, baking soda, cinnamon, salt, nutmeg and cardamom together. Heat
1/2 cup of the butter in a small saucepan until melted. Add the brown sugar. Cook
over low heat until smooth, stirring frequently. Remove from the heat. Let stand until
room temperature. Beat the remaining 3/4 cup butter, sugar and the cooled brown sugar
mixture in a large mixing bowl for 3 minutes or until smooth and light. Add the eggs
1 at a time, mixing well after each addition. Beat in 3/4 cup liqueur and the rum on
low speed. Fold in the sifted dry ingredients. Fold in the apples and pecans. Spoon into
a greased 10-inch tube pan.

Bake in a preheated 325-degree oven for 70 to 75 minutes or until a wooden pick
inserted in the center comes out clean. Cool in the pan for 10 minutes. Loosen the
cake from the sides of the pan and invert onto a platter. Pierce the top of the cake
several times with a long skewer. Sprinkle with 6 tablespoons liqueur. Pour Irish Cream
Glaze over the top of the warm cake, letting it drip down the sides. Let stand until
cooled completely. Let cake stand for 1 to 2 days for enhanced flavor.

Yield: 16 servings

IRISH CREAM GLAZE

2 cups confectioners' sugar

1/4 cup Irish cream liqueur

2 tablespoons (about) water

Combine the confectioners' sugar, liqueur and enough water to make a thin glaze in a
bowl and mix well.

FRESH BANANA CAKE

2 1/4 cups sifted cake flour
3/4 teaspoon baking soda
1/2 teaspoon baking powder
1/2 teaspoon salt
1 cup mashed overripe bananas
(about 2 large)
1/4 cup plain yogurt or
buttermilk
1 teaspoon vanilla extract
1/2 cup (1 stick) unsalted
butter, softened

1 cup sugar
2 eggs
8 ounces cream cheese,
softened
1/2 cup (1 stick) unsalted
butter, softened
2 teaspoons vanilla extract
1/8 teaspoon salt
1 (16-ounce) package
confectioners' sugar, sifted
2 to 3 large firm bananas

Sift the cake flour, baking soda, baking powder and 1/2 teaspoon salt together. Whisk the mashed bananas, yogurt and 1 teaspoon vanilla together in a bowl. Cream 1/2 cup butter and sugar in a mixing bowl until light and fluffy. Add the eggs 1 at a time, mixing well after each addition. Add the sifted dry ingredients alternately with the banana mixture beginning and ending with the dry ingredients, mixing just until combined after each addition; do not overmix.

Divide the batter evenly between two buttered and floured 8-inch round cake pans. Smooth the tops of the batter. Place one pan in the upper third and one pan in the lower third of a preheated 350-degree oven. Bake for 9 minutes. Switch the positions of the pans. Bake for 9 minutes or until cake springs back when lightly touched and a wooden pick inserted in the center comes out clean. Cool in the pans for 10 minutes. Loosen the cake layers from the edges. Invert layers onto a wire rack to cool completely. You may wrap the cooled layers in plastic wrap at this point and keep at room temperature for 1 day.

Beat the cream cheese and 1/2 cup butter in a mixing bowl until light and fluffy. Beat in 2 teaspoons vanilla and 1/8 teaspoon salt. Beat in the confectioners' sugar gradually. Beat until smooth.

Cut the firm bananas into diagonal slices. Place 1 cake layer on a serving plate. Spread a thin layer of frosting over the layer. Arrange the banana slices over the frosting, overlapping the slices slightly. Place the remaining cake layer on the bananas. Spread the remaining frosting over the top and side of the cake. May be kept for up to 8 hours at room temperature.

Yield: 12 servings

MOM'S CHOCOLATE CAKE

2 cups sugar
2 cups flour
1 teaspoon baking soda
1/2 teaspoon salt
1/2 cup shortening
3 tablespoons baking cocoa
1/2 cup (1 stick) butter
1 cup water
1/2 cup buttermilk
2 eggs
1 teaspoon vanilla extract
Chocolate Icing

Sift the sugar, flour, baking soda and salt together in a large bowl. Combine the shortening, baking cocoa, butter and water in a saucepan. Bring to a boil, stirring frequently. Pour over the sifted dry ingredients and mix well. Add the buttermilk, eggs and vanilla and mix well. Pour into a greased 9×13-inch baking pan. Bake at 325 degrees for 35 to 40 minutes or until a wooden pick inserted in the center comes out clean. Pour Chocolate Icing over the hot cake.

Yield: 15 servings

CHOCOLATE ICING

3 tablespoons baking cocoa
1/2 cup (1 stick) butter
6 tablespoons milk
1 (16-ounce) package confectioners' sugar, sifted
1 teaspoon vanilla extract
1 cup coarsely chopped pecans

Combine the baking cocoa, butter and milk in a saucepan. Bring to a boil, stirring frequently. Remove from the heat. Add the confectioners' sugar and vanilla and mix well. Stir in the pecans.

HEAVENLY HASH CAKE

1 cup (2 sticks) margarine
1/4 cup baking cocoa
4 eggs
2 cups sugar
1 1/2 cups self-rising flour
1 teaspoon vanilla extract
1 cup chopped pecans
1 (10-ounce) package marshmallows
Chocolate Glaze
Pecans

Heat the margarine and baking cocoa in a large saucepan until margarine is melted, stirring frequently. Beat the eggs and sugar in a mixing bowl. Add to the margarine mixture. Add the flour and vanilla and mix well. Stir in the chopped pecans. Pour into a greased 9X13-inch baking pan. Bake at 350 degrees for 35 minutes. Arrange the marshmallows over the top of the cake. Let stand until completely cool. Spread Chocolate Glaze over the marshmallows. Arrange the pecans over the top.

Yield: 15 servings

CHOCOLATE GLAZE

1 (16-ounce) package confectioners' sugar
1/4 cup (1/2 stick) butter, softened
1/4 cup baking cocoa
Milk

Combine the confectioners' sugar, butter, baking cocoa and enough milk to make of a spreading consistency in a bowl and mix well.

HONEY BUN CAKE

1 (2-layer) package yellow cake mix
4 eggs
3/4 cup vegetable oil
1 cup sour cream
1/2 cup (1 stick) margarine, melted
1 cup packed brown sugar
1 tablespoon cinnamon
1 cup chopped pecans
21/2 cups confectioners' sugar
1 teaspoon vanilla extract
1/4 cup milk

Combine the cake mix, eggs, oil and sour cream in a mixing bowl. Beat for 4 minutes or until smooth and creamy. Pour into a greased and floured 9X13-inch baking pan.

Combine the margarine, brown sugar, cinnamon and pecans in a bowl and mix well. Pour over the batter. Cut into the batter with a knife, creating a swirl effect. Bake at 325 degrees for 40 minutes.

Combine the confectioners' sugar, vanilla and milk in a bowl and mix until smooth. Spread over the hot cake.

Yield: 15 servings

ITALIAN LOVE CAKE

2 pounds ricotta cheese
4 eggs
3/4 cup sugar
1 teaspoon vanilla extract
1 (2-layer) package marble cake mix
Pudding Frosting

Combine the ricotta cheese, eggs, sugar and vanilla in a bowl and mix well.

Prepare the cake mix using the package directions. Pour into a greased and floured 9×13-inch baking pan. Spread the ricotta cheese mixture over the batter. Bake in a preheated 350-degree oven for 70 minutes. Let stand for 3 hours.

Spread Pudding Frosting over the top of the cooled cake.

Yield: 15 servings

PUDDING FROSTING

1 (4-ounce) package chocolate instant pudding mix
1 cup milk
8 ounces nondairy whipped topping

Combine the pudding mix and milk in a bowl and mix well. Stir in the whipped topping.

LEMON POUND CAKE

2 cups (4 sticks) butter
2 (16-ounce) packages confectioners' sugar
8 eggs
2 cups cake flour
Juice of 1/2 lemon
1^1/$_2$ teaspoons grated lemon zest
Lemon Glaze

Cream the butter in a mixing bowl until light and fluffy. Beat in the sugar. Add the eggs 1 at a time, mixing well after each addition. Add the cake flour and mix well. Stir in the lemon juice and lemon zest. Pour the batter into a greased and floured 10-inch tube pan.

Bake at 325 degrees for 1 hour and 20 minutes. Cool in the pan for 5 minutes. Invert onto a serving plate. Pour Lemon Glaze over the warm cake.

Yield: 16 servings

LEMON GLAZE

Juice from 1^1/$_2$ lemons
1/2 (16-ounce) package confectioners' sugar

Combine the lemon juice and confectioners' sugar in a bowl and mix until smooth and creamy.

CREAM CHEESE POUND CAKE

1 (2-layer) package yellow cake mix
1/2 cup sugar
8 ounces cream cheese, softened
2 tablespoons butter
1/2 cup vegetable oil
1/2 cup hot water
4 eggs

Combine the cake mix, sugar, cream cheese, butter, oil, water and eggs in a mixing bowl. Beat for 4 minutes or until smooth and creamy. Pour into a greased bundt pan. Bake at 325 degrees for 25 to 30 minutes or until a wooden pick inserted in the center comes out clean. Cool in the pan for 10 minutes. Invert onto a serving plate.

Yield: 16 servings

POPPY SEED CAKE

1 (2-layer) package yellow cake mix
1 cup water
1/2 cup vegetable oil
1 (4-ounce) package coconut instant pudding mix
4 eggs
1 tablespoon (heaping) poppy seeds
1 teaspoon vanilla extract
1 cup confectioners' sugar
3 tablespoons lemon juice

Beat the cake mix, water, oil and pudding mix in a mixing bowl for 1 minute. Add the eggs 1 at a time, beating for 1 minute after each addition. Add the poppy seeds and vanilla and mix well. Pour into a greased and floured bundt or 10-inch tube pan. Bake at 350 degrees for 40 to 45 minutes or until a wooden pick inserted in the center comes out clean. Cool in the pan for 10 minutes. Invert onto a serving plate.

Combine the confectioners' sugar and lemon juice in a bowl and mix until smooth. Drizzle over the warm cake.

Yield: 16 servings

MANDARIN ORANGE CAKE

MANDARIN ORANGE CAKE

1 (2-layer) package yellow cake mix
3/4 cup vegetable oil
3 eggs
1 (11-ounce) can mandarin oranges
Pineapple Icing

Combine the cake mix, oil, eggs and oranges in a bowl and mix well. Pour into 3 greased and floured 8-inch round cake pans.

Bake at 350 degrees for 30 to 35 minutes or until a wooden pick inserted in the center comes out clean. Cool in the pans for 10 minutes. Remove to a wire rack to cool completely. Spread Pineapple Icing between the layers and over the top and side of the cooled cake. May garnish with additional mandarin oranges.

Yield: 16 servings

PINEAPPLE ICING

1 (20-ounce) can crushed pineapple, drained
1 (4-ounce) package instant vanilla pudding mix
1 teaspoon vanilla extract
16 ounces nondairy whipped topping

Combine the pineapple and pudding mix in a bowl and mix well. Stir in the vanilla. Fold in the whipped topping.

OATMEAL CAKE

1¹/3 cups flour
1 teaspoon baking soda
1/2 teaspoon salt
1¹/2 cups hot water
1 cup rolled oats
1 cup sugar
1 cup packed brown sugar
1 cup vegetable oil
2 eggs
Brown Sugar Icing

Sift the flour, baking soda and salt together. Combine the hot water and oats in a large bowl. Let stand for 5 minutes. Add the sugar, brown sugar and oil to the oats and mix well. Add the eggs and mix well. Add the sifted dry ingredients and mix well; batter will be thin. Pour into a 9×13-inch baking pan. Bake at 300 degrees for 45 to 60 minutes or until a wooden pick inserted in the center comes out clean.

Spread Brown Sugar Icing over the hot cake. Bake for 5 minutes longer.

Yield: 15 servings

BROWN SUGAR ICING

1 cup packed brown sugar
1/2 cup (1 stick) butter
1/2 cup evaporated milk
1 cup chopped nuts
1 cup flaked coconut

Combine the brown sugar, butter and milk in a saucepan. Bring to a boil, stirring frequently. Boil for 1 minute. Stir in the nuts and coconut.

PUMPKIN PIE CAKE

1 (16-ounce) can pumpkin
2 teaspoons cinnamon
3 eggs
1 (5-ounce) can evaporated milk
1 cup sugar
1 (2-layer) butter cake mix
1 cup pecans
3/4 cup (1½ sticks) margarine
8 ounces nondairy whipped topping

Combine the pumpkin and cinnamon in a bowl and mix well. Add the eggs 1 at a time, mixing well after each addition. Add the milk and sugar and mix well. Pour into a buttered 9×13-inch baking pan.

Crumble the cake mix over the layer. Sprinkle the pecans over the cake mix. Heat the margarine in a saucepan until melted. Drizzle over the pecans. Bake at 350 degrees for 1 hour. Serve with the whipped topping.

Yield: 15 servings

PUMPKIN ROLL

3/4 cup flour
1 teaspoon baking powder
1 teaspoon cinnamon
1/2 teaspoon salt
3 eggs
1 cup sugar
2/3 cup pumpkin
Pecan pieces
Confectioners' sugar
Cream Cheese Filling

Combine the flour, baking powder, cinnamon and salt in a bowl and mix well. Beat the eggs in a mixing bowl for 5 minutes gradually adding the sugar. Fold in the pumpkin. Add the flour mixture gradually, mixing well after each addition. Pour into a greased and floured 10x15-inch jelly roll pan. Sprinkle with pecans. Bake at 375 degrees for 15 minutes.

Dust a clean kitchen towel with confectioners' sugar. Invert the cake onto the towel. Roll the warm cake in the towel as for a jelly roll from the short side and place on a wire rack to cool.

Unroll the cooled cake carefully and remove the towel. Spread Cream Cheese Filling to the edge and reroll. Place seam side down on a serving plate. Chill, covered, for 2 hours.

Yield: 8 to 10 servings

CREAM CHEESE FILLING

1 cup confectioners' sugar
1/4 cup (1/2 stick) butter, softened
8 ounces cream cheese, softened
1/2 teaspoon vanilla extract
11/2 to 2 cups pecan pieces

Combine the confectioners' sugar, butter, cream cheese and vanilla in a bowl and mix until smooth. Stir in the pecans.

RED VELVET CAKE

2¹/4 cups cake flour,
sifted twice
¹/2 teaspoon salt
¹/2 cup shortening
1¹/2 cups sugar
2 eggs
3 bottles red food coloring

1 cup buttermilk
1 teaspoon vanilla extract
1 teaspoon baking soda
1 teaspoon vinegar
¹/2 teaspoon almond extract
Vanilla Frosting

Combine the cake flour and salt in a bowl and mix well. Beat the shortening and sugar in a mixing bowl until light and fluffy. Add the eggs 1 at a time, mixing well after each addition. Beat in the red food coloring. Add the flour mixture and buttermilk alternately, mixing well after each addition. Add the vanilla, baking soda, vinegar and almond extract and mix well. Pour into two greased and floured round cake pans.

Bake at 350 degrees for 30 minutes or until a wooden pick inserted in the center comes out clean. Cool in the pan for 10 minutes. Remove to a wire rack to cool completely. Spread Vanilla Frosting between the layers and over the top and side of the cooled cake.

Yield: 12 servings

VANILLA FROSTING

1 cup milk
¹/4 cup flour
1 cup sugar

1 cup shortening
1 teaspoon vanilla extract
Dash of salt

Combine the milk and flour in a saucepan and mix well. Cook until mixture thickens into a paste, stirring constantly. Chill until cooled completely.

Combine the sugar, shortening, vanilla and salt in a mixing bowl. Beat until light and fluffy. Add the cold flour mixture. Beat on high until light and fluffy.

RUM CAKE

1/2 cup chopped pecans
1 (2-layer) package yellow cake mix
1/2 cup light rum
1/2 cup water
1/2 cup vegetable oil
4 eggs
1 (4-ounce) package instant vanilla pudding mix
Rum Glaze

Grease and flour a bundt pan. Sprinkle the pecans over the bottom of the pan.

Combine the cake mix, rum, water, oil and eggs in a mixing bowl. Beat for 1 minute. Add the pudding mix. Beat for 2 minutes. Pour into the prepared pan. Bake in a preheated 350-degree oven for 50 to 60 minutes or until a wooden pick inserted in the center comes out clean.

Pour hot Rum Glaze over the hot cake. Let stand for 30 minutes. Invert onto a serving plate.

Yield: 15 servings

RUM GLAZE

1 cup sugar
1/2 cup (1 stick) butter
1/4 cup rum
1/4 cup water

Combine the sugar, butter, rum and water in a saucepan. Bring to a boil, stirring frequently. Boil for 2 to 3 minutes.

SOUR CREAM CAKE

1 (2-layer) package white cake mix
1 cup sour cream
1/2 cup sugar
3/4 cup vegetable oil
4 eggs
3 tablespoons brown sugar
3 tablespoons cinnamon
Confectioners' Sugar Glaze (optional)

Combine the cake mix, sour cream, sugar and oil in a mixing bowl and beat for 2 minutes or until smooth. Add the eggs 1 at a time, mixing well after each addition. Pour half of the batter into a tube pan. Sprinkle the brown sugar and cinnamon over the batter. Pour the remaining batter over the brown sugar and cinnamon.

Bake the cake at 350 degrees for 1 hour. Cool in the pan for 10 minutes. Invert onto a serving plate. Drizzle Confectioners' Sugar Glaze over the top.

Yield: 8 to 10 servings

CONFECTIONERS' SUGAR GLAZE

1 cup confectioners' sugar
3 tablespoons butter, softened
3 tablespoons (or more) milk

Beat the confectioners' sugar and butter in a mixing bowl until light and fluffy. Beat in the milk, adding additional milk as needed to make of a spreading consistency.

WHITE TEXAS SHEET CAKE

1 cup (2 sticks) butter or margarine
1 cup water
2 cups flour
2 cups sugar
2 eggs, beaten
1/2 cup sour cream
1 teaspoon salt
1 teaspoon baking soda
1 (8-ounce) can crushed pineapple, drained
Walnut Frosting

Combine the butter and water in a large saucepan. Bring to a boil, stirring frequently. Remove from the heat. Let stand until slightly cooled. Add the flour, sugar, eggs, sour cream, salt and baking soda and mix until smooth. Fold in the pineapple. Spoon into a greased 10X15-inch cake pan.

Bake at 375 degrees for 20 to 22 minutes or until cake is golden brown and a wooden pick inserted in the center comes out clean. Cool in the pan for 20 minutes. Spread Walnut Frosting over the top.

Yield: 16 to 20 servings

WALNUT FROSTING

1/2 cup (1 stick) butter or margarine
1/4 cup milk
41/2 cups confectioners' sugar
1 cup chopped walnuts or pecans

Combine the butter and milk in a saucepan. Bring to a boil, stirring frequently. Remove from the heat. Add the confectioners' sugar and mix until smooth. Stir in the walnuts.

CINNAMON ROLL BREAD PUDDING

6 to 8 day-old cinnamon rolls, torn into small pieces
1/3 cup raisins
1/3 cup chopped pecans
4 cups milk
5 eggs
1 cup sugar
1 teaspoon vanilla extract
1/4 cup (1/2 stick) butter or margarine
Vanilla Sauce

Arrange the cinnamon roll pieces evenly in a greased 9X13-inch baking dish. Sprinkle the raisins and pecans over the rolls. Beat the milk, eggs, sugar and vanilla in a bowl. Pour over the rolls. Chill, covered, for 8 to 12 hours.

Cut the butter into small pieces. Sprinkle over the top. Place the baking dish in a larger baking pan. Add enough water to the larger pan to come halfway up the sides of the baking dish. Bake in a preheated 350-degree oven for 40 to 45 minutes. Serve with Vanilla Sauce.

Yield: 15 servings

VANILLA SAUCE

1 1/3 cups heavy cream
1/2 cup sugar
4 egg yolks
1 teaspoon vanilla extract

Place the cream and 1/4 cup of the sugar in a double boiler over simmering water. Cook until heated through. Combine the remaining 1/4 cup sugar and the egg yolks in a bowl and mix well. Stir a small amount of the hot cream mixture into the egg yolk mixture. Stir the egg yolk mixture into the hot cream mixture. Cook for 8 to 10 minutes or until mixture thickens and coats a spoon, stirring constantly. Remove from the heat. Stir in the vanilla. Serve warm.

BEER CHEESECAKE

1¹/2 cups flour
6 tablespoons sugar
1 teaspoon grated lemon zest
1/2 cup (1 stick) margarine
2 egg yolks
1/2 teaspoon vanilla extract
Beer Filling

Combine the flour, sugar and lemon zest in a bowl. Cut in the margarine until crumbly. Stir in the egg yolks and vanilla. Chill for 30 minutes. Press 1/3 of the dough over the bottom of a springform pan, reserving the remaining dough. Bake in a preheated 425-degree oven for 8 to 10 minutes. Let stand until cool. Press the remaining dough up the side of the pan to within 1 inch of the top edge.

Pour the Beer Filling over the crust. Bake at 425 degrees for 10 minutes. Reduce the temperature to 300 degrees. Bake for 1 hour and 15 minutes or until top is firm and golden. Cool on a wire rack.

Yield: 8 to 10 servings

BEER FILLING

32 ounces cream cheese, softened
1 cup finely shredded very sharp Cheddar cheese
1/2 teaspoon grated lemon zest
1³/4 cups sugar
2 egg yolks
4 eggs
1/4 cup beer
1/4 cup heavy cream
1/2 teaspoon grated orange zest

Beat the cream cheese and Cheddar cheese at high speed in a mixing bowl for 5 minutes. Beat in the lemon zest, sugar, egg yolks, eggs, beer, heavy cream and orange zest at medium speed.

ELEGANT RICH CHEESECAKE

1¹/2 cups graham cracker crumbs
¹/4 cup sugar
¹/2 cup (1 stick) butter or margarine, melted
24 ounces cream cheese, softened
1¹/2 cups sugar
¹/8 teaspoon salt
4 eggs
1 teaspoon vanilla extract
2 cups sour cream
¹/4 cup sugar
2 teaspoons vanilla extract
Sliced strawberries for garnish

Combine the graham cracker crumbs, ¹/4 cup sugar and butter in a bowl and mix well. Press over the bottom and up the side to within 1 inch of the top edge of a buttered 9-inch springform pan. Chill until ready to use.

Beat the cream cheese in a mixing bowl until smooth. Add 1¹/2 cups sugar and mix well. Add the salt. Beat until light and fluffy. Add the eggs 1 at a time, mixing well after each addition. Beat in 1 teaspoon vanilla. Pour into the prepared crust. Bake at 350 degrees for 50 minutes or until set. Let stand for 15 minutes. Increase the oven temperature to 450 degrees.

Combine the sour cream, ¹/4 cup sugar and 2 teaspoons vanilla in a bowl and mix well. Spread over the top of the cheesecake. Bake for 10 minutes or until topping is set. Cool on a wire rack. Chill in the refrigerator. Loosen the cheesecake from the edge. Garnish with strawberries. You may add ¹/2 cup baking cocoa to the topping to make a chocolate topping.

Yield: 10 servings

CHERRY DELIGHT

1 cup flour
1/2 cup pecans
1/2 cup (1 stick) margarine
1/4 cup packed brown sugar
8 ounces cream cheese, softened
1 cup confectioners' sugar
1 teaspoon vanilla extract
16 ounces nondairy whipped topping
1 (21-ounce) can cherry pie filling

Combine the flour, pecans, margarine and brown sugar in a bowl and mix well. Press over the bottom of a 9×13-inch baking pan. Bake at 400 degrees for 10 to 15 minutes or until light brown. Let stand until slighty cooled. Crumble the crust in the pan.

Combine the cream cheese, confectioners' sugar and vanilla in a mixing bowl and beat until smooth. Fold in the whipped topping. Spread over the crust. Spread the pie filling over the cream cheese mixture. Chill, covered, for 12 hours or longer.

Yield: 12 servings

NAPOLEON CREAM PUFFS

1 cup water
1/2 cup (1 stick) margarine
1 cup flour
4 eggs
Napoleon Cream Filling

Bring the water and margarine to a boil in a saucepan. Stir in the flour. Cook over low heat for 1 minute or until mixture forms a ball, stirring constantly. Remove from the heat. Beat in the eggs; mixture will be sticky and smooth. Drop by 1/4 cupfuls 3 inches apart onto a baking sheet. Bake at 400 degrees for 35 to 40 minutes or until puffed and golden; do not open oven door for at least 30 minutes. Cool completely on the baking sheet.

Cut a cream puff in half lengthwise. Spoon Napoleon Cream Filling over one half. Top with the remaining half. Repeat with the remaining cream puffs.

Yield: 8 to 10 servings

NAPOLEON CREAM FILLING

3/4 cup sugar
1/4 cup cornstarch
1/8 teaspoon salt
1 1/2 cups milk
4 egg yolks
1 1/2 teaspoons vanilla extract
1/2 cup whipping cream, whipped

Combine the sugar, cornstarch and salt in a heavy saucepan and mix well. Stir in the milk. Cook over low heat until mixture thickens, stirring constantly. Beat the egg yolks in a bowl until thick and pale yellow. Stir a small amount of the hot milk mixture into the beaten egg yolks. Stir the egg yolks into the hot milk mixture. Cook until mixture thickens, stirring constantly. Remove from the heat. Stir in the vanilla. Cover the filling with waxed paper. Chill in the refrigerator. Fold in the whipped cream.

CUBAN FLAN

2 cups sugar
8 eggs
2 cups sugar
2 tablespoons vanilla extract
2 (12-ounce) cans evaporated milk

Heat 2 cups sugar in a skillet until melted, stirring constantly. Pour into a 2- to 3-pound empty coffee can, rotating the can to coat the bottom and 1/3 of the way up the side. Run under cold water until sugar hardens. Beat the eggs in a mixing bowl. Beat in 2 cups sugar, vanilla and evaporated milk. Pour over the hardened sugar. Cover the can with foil. Place in a larger baking pan. Add enough water to the larger pan to fill halfway. Bake at 350 degrees for 11/2 to 2 hours or until a knife inserted in the center comes out clean. Cool on a wire rack. Chill for 8 to 12 hours. Invert flan onto a serving dish. Serve with whipped cream. You may halve the ingredients in this recipe and bake in a 1-pound coffee can.

Yield: 6 to 8 servings

FRUIT THAIS

1 (16-ounce) can each sliced peaches, pears, apricots,
pineapple chunks and pitted dark cherries, drained, chopped
1 pound bananas, chopped
1/2 cup sherry
1/2 cup packed brown sugar
1/2 cup almond slivers
Pats of butter
1 package coconut macaroons, crumbled

Combine the peaches, pears, apricots, pineapple, cherries and bananas in a 9X13-inch dish. Pour the sherry over the fruit. Let stand for 2 to 12 hours; drain. Layer the fruit, brown sugar, almonds, butter and macaroons half at a time in a 9X13-inch baking dish. Bake at 350 degrees for 20 minutes.

Yield: 10 to 15 servings

WHITE CHOCOLATE MOUSSE WITH RED RASPBERRY COULIS

1 teaspoon unflavored gelatin
1/4 cup cold water
1/4 cup milk
5 ounces white chocolate, broken into pieces
1 1/2 cups whipping cream
Red Raspberry Coulis
Raspberries for garnish

Soften the gelatin in the cold water in a glass dish. Microwave on High for 20 to 40 seconds. Let stand for 2 minutes or until gelatin is dissolved. Bring the milk to the simmering point in a saucepan. Remove from the heat. Add the white chocolate and stir until chocolate is melted and mixture is smooth. Stir in the gelatin. Chill for 10 minutes or until thickened.

Beat the whipping cream in a mixing bowl until stiff peaks form. Fold in the white chocolate mixture. Alternate layers of Red Raspberry Coulis and the mousse in 4 tall parfait glasses until all ingredients are used. Chill for 1 to 2 hours. Garnish with raspberries.

Yield: 4 servings

RED RASPBERRY COULIS

2 (10-ounce) packages frozen raspberries in syrup
Juice of 1/2 lemon
1/4 cup sugar
2 tablespoons cornstarch
1/2 cup cold water
1 tablespoon Grand Marnier

Purée the raspberries and lemon juice in a food processor or blender. Strain, pressing with the back of a spoon. Combine the strained juice, sugar, cornstarch, water and Grand Marnier in a saucepan and mix well. Bring to a boil over medium heat, stirring frequently. Reduce the heat. Cook for 1 minute, stirring constantly. Remove from the heat. Let stand until ready to use.

FRENCH PASTRY

2 cups flour
1 cup (2 sticks) margarine, melted
1 tablespoon sugar
Strawberry Filling

Combine the flour, margarine and sugar in a bowl and mix well. Press over the bottom and up the sides of a 9x9-inch baking pan. Bake at 350 degrees for 20 minutes. Cool on a wire rack.

Spoon Strawberry Filling into the crust. Chill, covered, for 3 hours or longer.

Yield: 9 servings

STRAWBERRY FILLING

1 (14-ounce) can sweetened condensed milk
1/3 cup lemon juice
16 ounces nondairy whipped topping
2 (10-ounce) packages frozen strawberries, thawed, drained

Combine the milk, lemon juice, whipped topping and strawberries in a bowl and mix well.

RICE PUDDING

1/4 cup (1/2 stick) margarine

3 eggs

1 cup sugar

4 cups milk

2 1/2 cups cooked rice

2 teaspoons vanilla extract

1/2 teaspoon salt

3/4 teaspoon nutmeg

3/4 cup raisins

Place the margarine in a 2-quart round baking dish. Heat in a 300-degree oven until melted. Remove from the oven.

Beat the eggs in a mixing bowl. Beat in the sugar gradually. Add the milk, rice, vanilla, salt and nutmeg and mix well. Pour into the prepared dish. Sprinkle the raisins over the top. Bake for 35 to 40 minutes or until pudding is set.

Yield: 15 servings

BLACK CHERRY PUDDING

1 (16-ounce) can black bing cherries
1 cup flour
1 cup sugar
1 teaspoon baking soda
1 egg, beaten
1 tablespoon butter, melted
1 cup chopped nuts
Cream Sauce

Drain the cherries, reserving the juice. Combine the flour, sugar, baking soda, egg and butter in a bowl and mix well. Stir in the cherries. Add enough of the reserved cherry juice to make a very thick batter. Stir in the nuts. Spoon into a shallow 7×12-inch baking dish. Bake at 350 degrees for 30 minutes or until firm. Serve warm with Cream Sauce.

Yield: 8 servings

CREAM SAUCE

1 cup sugar
1/2 cup (1 stick) butter
1/2 cup cream
1 teaspoon vanilla extract

Place the sugar, butter, cream and vanilla in a double boiler over boiling water. Cook until thickened, stirring frequently. Serve warm.

GRAND MARNIER SOUFFLE

2 tablespoons sugar

1/4 cup cornstarch

1/4 cup sugar

Pinch of salt

1 1/2 tablespoons butter

5 ounces milk

2 1/4 teaspoons grated orange zest

3 egg yolks, beaten

4 1/2 teaspoons Grand Marnier

4 egg whites

Pinch of cream of tartar

2 tablespoons sugar

St. Cecilia's Sauce

Butter the side and bottom of a 22-ounce soufflé dish. Sprinkle with 2 tablespoons sugar. Combine the cornstarch, 1/4 cup sugar and salt in a bowl and mix well. Combine the butter and milk in a saucepan. Stir in the cornstarch mixture and the orange zest. Cook over medium heat until mixture thickens, stirring constantly. Remove from the heat. Stir a small amount of the hot mixture into the egg yolks. Stir the egg yolks into the hot mixture. Stir in the Grand Marnier.

Beat the egg whites and cream of tartar in a mixing bowl until soft peaks form. Add 2 tablespoons sugar gradually, beating until stiff peaks form. Fold half into the egg yolk mixture. Beat the remaining egg whites briefly. Fold into the egg yolk mixture. Pour into the prepared dish. Place the dish in a larger baking pan. Add enough water to the larger pan to fill halfway. Bake in a preheated 400-degree oven for 60 to 65 minutes. Serve immediately with St. Cecilia's Sauce.

Yield: 4 servings

ST. CECILIA'S SAUCE

2 egg yolks

(See Editor's Note)

Pinch of salt

3/4 cup confectioners' sugar

1 cup whipping cream

2 tablespoons Grand Marnier

Beat the egg yolks in a mixing bowl until thick and pale yellow. Beat in the salt and confectioners' sugar. Beat the whipping cream in a mixing bowl until stiff peaks form. Fold into the egg yolk mixture. Stir in the Grand Marnier.

Editor's Note: To avoid raw eggs that may carry salmonella, use an equivalent amount of pasteurized egg substitute, or meringue powder, sometimes sold as powdered egg whites.

STRAWBERRY TORTE

1 cup sifted flour
1 teaspoon baking powder
1/4 teaspoon salt
1/2 cup (1 stick) butter, softened
1/2 cup sugar
5 egg yolks
1 teaspoon vanilla extract
3 tablespoons milk
5 egg whites
1/4 teaspoon almond extract
3/4 cup sugar
1/2 cup slivered almonds, toasted
2 cups whipping cream
1/4 cup sugar
1/2 teaspoon almond extract
2 pints strawberries, cut into quarters

Sift the flour, baking powder and salt together. Cream the butter and 1/2 cup sugar in a mixing bowl until light and fluffy. Add the egg yolks 1 at a time, mixing well after each addition. Beat in the vanilla and milk. Fold in the flour mixture. Spread evenly in two greased and floured 9-inch round pans.

Beat the egg whites with 1/4 teaspoon almond extract in a mixing bowl until foamy and doubled in volume. Sprinkle 3/4 cup sugar over the egg whites. Beat until sugar is dissolved and stiff peaks form. Spread evenly over the batter. Sprinkle the almonds over the egg whites. Bake at 350 degrees for 30 minutes or until meringue is light brown.

Cool baked layers in the pans for 5 minutes. Loosen the edges. Place, meringue sides up, on a wire rack. Let stand until completely cool.

Beat the whipping cream, 1/4 cup sugar and 1/2 teaspoon almond extract in a mixing bowl until stiff. Place 1 layer on a serving plate. Spread half of the whipping cream over the layer. Arrange half of the strawberries over the whipping cream. Place the remaining layer over the strawberries. Spread the remaining whipping cream over the layer. Arrange the remaining strawberries over the whipping cream.

Yield: 8 servings

BANANA PUDDING TRIFLE

1¹/3 cups sugar
3/4 cup flour
1/2 teaspoon salt
4 cups milk
8 egg yolks
1 tablespoon vanilla extract
1/4 cup bourbon
2 tablespoons rum
1 (12-ounce) package vanilla wafers
6 bananas, sliced
6 (1¹/2-ounce) English toffee candy bars, crushed
1 cup whipping cream
1 tablespoon confectioners' sugar

Combine the sugar, flour and salt in a saucepan and mix well. Whisk in the milk. Bring to a boil over medium heat, whisking constantly. Remove from the heat.

Beat the egg yolks in a mixing bowl until thick and pale yellow. Stir a small amount of the hot milk mixture into the beaten egg yolks. Stir the egg yolks into the hot mixture. Cook for 1 minute, stirring constantly. Remove from the heat. Stir the vanilla into the pudding.

Combine the bourbon and rum in a bowl and mix well. Layer 1/3 of the wafers, 1/3 of the bananas, 1/3 of the pudding and 1/4 of the crushed candy bars 3 times in a 4-quart dish, brushing the wafers with the bourbon mixture each time.

Beat the whipping cream at medium speed in a mixing bowl until foamy. Add the confectioners' sugar gradually, beating until soft peaks form. Spread over the trifle. Sprinkle the remaining crushed candy bars over the top. Chill, covered, for 3 hours.

Yield: 10 to 12 servings

CONTRIBUTOR LIST

Donna Anderson

Sharon Arnhart

Jo Arnold

Kim Arnold

Ginger Bailey

Heather Bailey

Linda Baldwin

Cindy Ball

Amy Beckett

Marzella Bender

Rosemary Boggs

Barbara Bradley

Patti Brady

Wanda Bright

Kelly Brown

Betty Brownlee

Cynthia Byrd

Melba Carter

Sherry Childress

Shanna Chudy

Alicia Chudy-Brown

Mary Lucy Collins

Lucille Cowan

Susan Dougan

Amy Dunn

Marilyn Eagan

Susan Eanes

Jean Edwards

June Edwards

Sharon Ferguson

E. G. Finch

Melanie Fischer

Carolyn Fisher

Deanna Fleming

Pam Glidewell

Marianne Gosser

Karen Hall

Lesa Hamm

Janet Herrell

Denise Hill

Mary Sue Hogue

Cathy Holderfield

Debbie Horton

Sandi Valli Howard

Jephrey Hubener

Kathy Jackson

Tanya Jacobs

Gladys Johnson

Lois Johnson

Juanita Jones

Margaret Ann Jordan

Alfred Keller

Mary Keller

Heather Kingston

Carolyn Kirkland	Lydia Palasota	Liz Thompson
Shirley Knox	Jan Pharo	Kris Tibbs
Frances Lance	Kay Phillips	Connie Vaden
Cathy Lay	Renee Pierce	Pat Wallace
Pat Lieggi	Damaris Porterfield	Mandy Ware
Shirley Loetscher	Kathy Primm	Velma Warner
Gaye Long	Ellowene Puttus	Beverly Watts
Jennifer Lowe	Risa Ratliff	Ellen Weiner
Evelyn McDonald	Sherron Regauld	Edwina Whalen-Aycock
Cheryl McKim	Ann Reynolds	Elaine White
Martha McNeil	Suzie Ridgely	Ginger White
Donna McNew	Lillian Sartin	Janis Williams
Martha Moore	Leslie Slattery	June Wilson
Brenda Morgan	Virginia Smith	Dean Wingfield
Lynda Neel	Barbara St. Onge	Ravenel Wright
Julie Nichols	Angela Stroud	Rhonda Zahnen
Natalie Oberle	Kara Swayne	
Sam Oberle	Hope Tanner	

INDEX

Natural Temptations

A Collection of Recipes from
The Junior League of North Little Rock
P.O. Box 9043
North Little Rock, Arkansas 72119

Please send me _____ copies of **Natural Temptations** at $21.95 each $ _____

Arkansas residents add 7.125% sales tax at $1.56 each $ _____

Shipping and handling at $2.00 each $ _____

Total $ _____

_____
Name

_____
Street Address

_____
City   State   Zip

_____
Daytime Telephone   Evening Telephone

Method of Payment: [   ] MasterCard   [   ] VISA

[   ] Check payable to the Junior League of North Little Rock

_____
Account Number   Expiration Date

_____
Signature

Photocopies will be accepted.